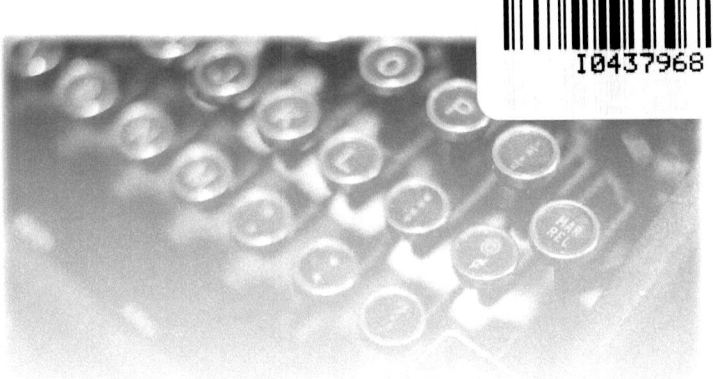

TAKE A LOOK INSIDE...

...AND DISCOVER SOME OF
OUR INDIVIDUALIZED CREATIVE
BOOK INTERIOR DESIGNS

Julie Ann James

Publisher/Founder/Project Facilitator
peppertreepublishing@yahoo.com

Teri Lynn Franco

Editorial Director/Office Manager
tfranco@peppertreepublishing.com

the Peppertree Press

Sarasota, Florida

For information regarding permission,
call 941-922-2662 or contact us at our website:
www.peppertreepublishing.com or write to:
the Peppertree Press, LLC.
Attention: Publisher
1269 First Street, Suite 7
Sarasota, Florida 34236

ISBN: 978-1-61493-511-7

Printed November 2017

~EXAMPLES OF~

Chapter Books

WILLIAM J. WARNER

HOLDUP NUMBER SIX

An FBI Novel Based On Actual Events

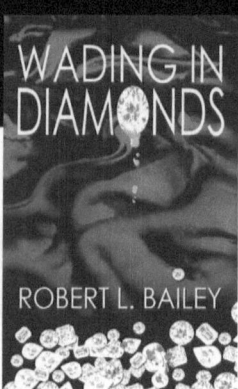

WADING IN DIAMONDS

ROBERT L. BAILEY

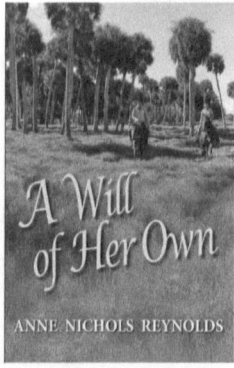

A Will of Her Own

ANNE NICHOLS REYNOLDS

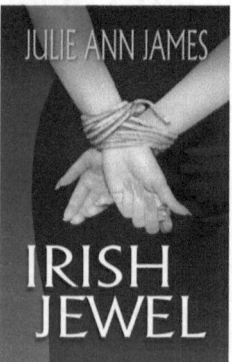

JULIE ANN JAMES

IRISH JEWEL

LORENZO'S RULES:
LORD OF THE NINTH UNDERWORLD

STEWART STEARNS

WILLIAM J. WARNER

HOLDUP
NUMBER
SIX

An FBI Novel Based On Actual Events

1
ATLANTA, 1988

As he rubbed his finger around the end of the barrel he felt a sharp prick. "Geez Wheezy, you'd a done good to file this off some more."

"Whutch'ya got, a burr?"

"Blood too, man."

"Well, you ain't s'posed to be foolin' with the business end anyway. You ough'ta know that. How long have you been workin' security?"

"Since '86, but I ain't never handled a shotgun before. Especially one that been sawed off."

"You best make friends with it, Junior. All you got to do is aim and fire. Rack it back hard like I showed ya 'n, fire again. You got more slugs in your pocket. You shouldn't need more than a couple if they fire back at all. Not likely to once they see a shotgun aimed at 'em."

"Yeah. Hope you right man. This is serious here." Bo West Jr. sat in the passenger seat of a cherry-red 1984 Oldsmobile Cutlass Supreme his brother stole from over in Birmingham. That fact alone bothered him. But he got used to living on the wrong side of the law. He was known by his brother, family, and friends as Bo. Those who "used" him called him Junior. On this day, he would be Junior.

"Just relax," said Wheezy. "This thing'll go. You just gotta' get out, shout, be firm, show a mean spirit. With that shotgun and all, and me and mine, they ain't gonna' do battle. I'm tellin' ya. Once you scare 'em you're in control."

Junior looked up through the rain-spattered windshield. The day was gloomy and dark as the last of a series of thunderstorms passed over Atlanta. His face was black, round, and pudgy, much like Wheezy's. He sported a gold tooth, which glistened when he smiled. Not exactly clean-shaven, Junior was good enough to pass muster whenever he donned the security guard's uniform to work the night shift at Peachtree Memorial, entrusted to protect the patients, staff, and people visiting a major metropolitan hospital.

He felt he was taking a step up here. He wouldn't have the security job long. Today's escapade would set the tone for his future. He wasn't wearing his uniform today—just jeans and a mechanic's shirt from a previous job, a black leather jacket, and a navy blue skullcap. It was mid-December, with a chill in the air, and Junior's breath left a fog on the side window. Like a child he took his finger and made symbols on the window before the moisture dissipated. His left hand kept tapping the stock of the shotgun. A half-broken-down Sunoco sign was bumping the pole it was attached to overhead.

Wheezy had chosen this vacant fuel-station parking lot to sit and wait on the truck from Georgia Armored to arrive a half block away at South Fulton Bank. While they waited, Junior's coffee grew cold. He chose not to drink it, as he didn't want to have to pee in the middle of the action. He'd rather shiver. Despite the chill, beads of sweat began to appear on the side of his face where his wannabe sideburns grew.

Wheezy noticed Junior's distress. "I've got confidence in you, man. You can do this. We'll be between the courier and the truck just like that. He'll never know we're comin' and he won't have time to react. Remember, we're just gettin' his satchel. We ain't taken down the whole truck. Takes too long. Driver dudn't pack, he stays in the truck. You don't have to worry about him. By the time he calls for help and help comes, we'll be gone. Long gone. Money, too. And that courier guard will be standin' there with crap in his pants."

"I just don't want anybody to get hurt. You know what I mean?"

"We've been through that. Ain't gonna happen."

"You sure driver don't pack?"

"No. Now listen. We've been through that like I said. Remember? I know people who have worked for them. He stays in the truck."

"And if the other guy draw—"

"What did I say about that?"

"Yeah, action beat reaction."

"That's right. That's what I've been tryin' to get through that thick skull of yours. Now you're all beadin' up sweat and tappin' away."

"Yeah, I know that's what you say. Action beat reaction, action beat reaction. I heard it enough. You've been trained to know. You know what the cops will do—when they come and what to expect. It's different for me."

"Wait a minute, you're no virgin. You've been through the system."

"Not for nothin' like this though."

"Okay Junior. You wanna back out now's your chance. No harm, no foul, no hurt feelings. Once we roll, we roll with it though, okay? You good?"

Junior took a long sigh. More fog on the window. With his finger he scribbled into the fog. "I good." He looked back at Wheezy and said, "My baby needs the money" and flashed his gold-toothed grin feigning concession.

The clock radio said 10:30 am. The noise of the morning rush hour had faded as people settled into their daily routines. Wheezy and Junior had been sitting under the Sunoco sign for thirty minutes, waiting patiently. Wheezy had followed Georgia Armored several times over the course of the last two months to get a read on their route and times— somewhat unpredictable but always between ten and eleven o'clock the truck would stop each Monday morning at this bank. They need to vary their routine, Wheezy thought, but since they won't, we'll take advantage. He had thought this through more than a few times.

As the rain eased off, it was eerily quiet. The only noise for the last half hour had been the constant eek-slap, eek-slap of the annoying sign overhead. Junior fumbled for a cigarette. Wheezy could tell Junior was wondering how he'd let himself get talked into this, but he had come to trust him, sort of, from his days working with him and for his ole man at Evins Wrecker Service.

"So when did you start smokin'?" Wheezy asked.

"So just now. Why?"

The roar of a big engine broke the silence. Wheezy recognized the sound and looked up. "Put it down, here it comes."

Junior missed his pocket and dropped both the cigarette and the lighter on the floor.

"Be cool now, we're gonna wait 'till he turns in and then we'll pull through the grocery store lot out of sight of the driver." Wheezy slipped the car into drive and moved out, cutting the radio off. Within a minute he was into the adjacent lot on the south side of the bank. He paused the car along a curb.

The truck had stopped on the north side. The courier was out in an instant and into the bank.

"The trick is to see the dude through the window as he starts to leave." Whispered Wheezy. "As soon as he starts for the door, we'll pull around the back of the bank. We've got to catch him after he comes out in no man's land before he gets back in the truck."

WADING
IN DIAMONDS

BY

ROBERT L. BAILEY

1.

His Delta flight landed at New York Kennedy at 12:33 p.m. He picked up one checked bag and caught a taxi to an address on 47th street between Fifth Avenue and Sixth Avenue.

This is the home of New York's diamond district which dates back to the 1930s when thousands of Orthodox Jews who worked in the diamond industry moved to New York's Midtown for the safety of New York, fleeing Belgium and the Netherlands to escape the Nazis. Today some 2,600 businesses are located in New York, all involved in some phase of the diamond business.

He walked to a U. S. Post Office on 47th between 3rd Avenue and Lexington, checked a post office box in the name of Rodney Williams and removed three large envelopes, all mailed International First Class to Williams. Each envelope contained a customs form showing the contents as "costume jewelry" with values ranging from $290 to $385.

Moving a few steps, he opened another box and removed four parcels addressed to Catherine Hyman. The customs form said the parcels contained costume jewelry valued at between $360 and $385.

He now had in his possession nine parcels—seven delivered

by mail, two delivered in person (one in his checked bag, one in his carry-on, neither of which was questioned by customs officials).

He entered the office of Esteem Diamond Cutters on 47th Street. Some of the more substantial diamond merchants have moved to an elaborate new 34-story building providing occupants prestige and safety. The new building is equipped with 350 security cameras, iris scanners, four finger prints of every visitor taken at the front desk, and tracking technology to assure that people authorized to enter the building go only where they are cleared to go.

Esteem Diamond Cutters, on the other hand, is not a prestige operation. Its 400 square foot office is located in a low-rise building that hasn't been upgraded since the 40s.

The Esteem receptionist knew him as Wade. No one knew his last name. And no one knew if Wade was his real first name. He often joked that it meant Wild Ass Diamond Expert. She led him to the office of Dieter Grunewald, president of Esteem, whom he had visited on several occasions over the years.

They didn't greet one another. The atmosphere was cold and unfriendly. Grunewald spoke first. "What have you got?"

"Here are $8.5 million of 'D' grade flawless rough diamonds. As with our previous arrangements, they are yours for $4.25 million.

Each rough diamond had been pressed into rings and bracelets made of a cardboard-like composite material produced by a 3-D printing process. 3-D printing has progressed to the point it is being used by auto manufacturers to produce replacement parts, jet engine parts, even human body parts, and by toy makers in creating nearly every toy being manufactured today. It's an ideal way to disguise expensive diamonds as cheap costume jewelry, avoiding taxes and the prying eyes of customs agents.

Grunewald didn't answer. He took the diamonds to his bench and examined each through his monocular loupe.

He returned 20 minutes later and said, "I'll give you $3 million."

"That's not what we agreed to. It's 50% of wholesale—all cash. That's $4.25 million."

"You must not hear well. I said $3 million, take it or leave it."

"You have left me no other choice. I'll leave it," as he began to repackage the rough diamonds. "We have contacts with many other diamond cutters who will appreciate the value we offer."

"Wait a minute. $3.25 million."

Wade continued to package the rough diamonds.

"OK, $3.5 million."

Wade said nothing, as he prepared to leave.

"OK, you win. I'll have $4.25 million cash for you. Tomorrow. Leave the diamonds so I can inspect them more carefully."

"It's $4.25 million. And I'll deliver the diamonds to you tomorrow when you hand me the money. I'll have additional diamonds for you at the same price whenever you have a need for them—say, in 30 days."

Grunewald didn't answer.

A Will of Her Own

BY

ANNE NICHOLS REYNOLDS

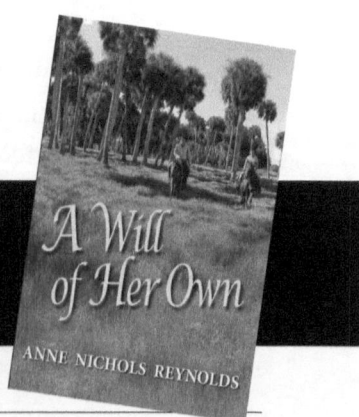

CHAPTER ONE

Katie Mulholland sat ramrod straight as she gave herself a no non-sense lecture to keep her mind on driving. This was a futile exercise because, in truth, she felt as wretched as the weather. The gray sky darkened to a purple bruise. Strong gusts of wind buffeted the blue Taurus and strewed broken limbs and clumps of gray moss across the empty two-lane road. White hot shards of lightning fractured the darkness and burst in a macabre dance above the treetops.

Thoughts of Gunnar's insistence on living together without marriage went against the values her parents had instilled in their children. She heard again her mother's admonition, "If you don't respect yourself, how can you expect others to respect you?"

Gunnar had one more year of law school and was adamant about not being pressured into marriage until he took a position in his father's law firm. Katie had met his parents once. They broadly hinted that a live-in arrangement was more amenable to them than marriage at this point in Gunnar's career. They hadn't said she was socially unacceptable, but their body language fairly shouted their disappointment.

A cold splash hit Katie when his mother snidely remarked, "We understand hormones, dear. Just be careful. You comprehend what I mean, don't you, dear?" His mother nodded as if believing Katie got the message. "There now, we understand one another."

The embarrassing comments provoked Katie to respond.

Gunnar accurately read the rising storm and jumped into the breach. "Mother, you're out of line. Katie's a nice girl, and I want her to be treated as such."

Katie was grateful for his words and the arm he had placed protectively around her shoulders. She swallowed her retort.

His mother had shrugged eloquently, and the bemused expression she cast her immaculately groomed husband was far from apologetic. The evening had been disastrous, and Gunnar was moody for days. "They'll learn to love you, as I do," he told her. This was the only time he mentioned love.

At least Katie's family had been warm and friendly, making Gunnar feel at home. They trusted Katie's judgment. Katie knew her parents would be disappointed if she moved in with Gunnar.

Katie longed to be home. She would miss the little apartment her parents helped her find near school, so she wouldn't have the distraction of dorm life. Her little abode had once housed the horses of the Delacroix family. The stable had been restored and turned into an apartment. Two maiden ladies, heiresses of the Delacroix line, kept their eyes on her comings and goings across the courtyard. Katie loved the rustic rooms that displayed her romantic décor, and the French Provencal eclectic mix of furniture. Her upright piano was the focal point, by way of, taking up the most space. Katie's music lifted her spirits and relaxed her.

Gunnar's larger apartment, a condo on Beecher Street, had a view of the swimming pool two floors below. His taste ran to stark Danish blond furniture, angular lines, and neutral colors. The uncluttered, pristine atmosphere suited the sophisticated Gunnar Andre Lindgren. He was a modern Viking, a masterful, suave intellectual who teased her about her naïve idealism and her romance novels. He was a devotee of Dvorsak, she of Chopin, but they found common ground in jazz. Katie was churched, and Gunnar dismissed religion as a crutch. His unbelief bothered her the most. Her faith was the cornerstone of her existence. Her mental list of pros and cons to the relationship was lopsided because they were opposites in many ways. Gunnar was handsome and on track to a great future. Katie knew part of the attraction was pride. He had pursued *her*. Katie's problem was not being comfortable with the idea of living with Gunnar. Liking someone and living with them were two different things. Adjustments and compromises were involved. Gunnar dominated. His superior attitude might be a deterrent to her growth as an individual.

A visit to the home of her older sister, Myra, had only confirmed she and Gunnar were mismatched. Katie wanted a marriage like Myra's, a husband like Paul to cherish her, and a couple of children to complete their lives. She and Myra were close, and on this last visit, she shared with her the hopes for her future and her fears of losing Gunnar. Confiding in Myra had always been easy.

Gunnar had given her an ultimatum after she stopped him during a sexually charged moment. He shook his head frustrated by her denial. "We can't go on like this. I'm not made out of stone. Grow up, Katie." His nostrils flared with passion, his sculptured lips drew back in a cynical smile, and his grey eyes glinted. Gunnar reclined away from her, his elbow on the arm of the couch, his other arm extended across its back. "Katie, Katie," he laughed with a touch of scorn.

"I want you. I need you, sweetheart," not "I love you." *He's too proud to say it, to get what he wants.* He looked so handsome with his blond hair swept across a broad forehead. Katie had felt stinging humiliation and despair as she buttoned her blouse. *Why can't I give myself to Gunnar? Because I'm not sure, not ready? Will I ever be?*

"You're all grown up now. You can make your own choices." His hands cupped her face, his thumbs rhythmically rubbing her cheeks. This was his way of saying her upbringing shouldn't matter, and he made her feel like a child. "You want this as much as I do."

Only she didn't. His seduction didn't feel right. Would she ever be totally comfortable with him? She knew the answer. *Why beat myself up over it? Because of pride, fear of failure?*

"I think you have some reservations about building a life with Gunnar," Myra had said. "You aren't comfortable with his lifestyle, and you're afraid he isn't going to change. And he won't change," she said emphatically, "but *you* will … if you want your marriage to succeed. Are you willing to compromise?"

Can I give up my beliefs, my identity for a future with Gunnar?

"You and Gunnar aren't in love. You're attracted to one another. There's a lot of territory between the two," Myra stated. "Real love doesn't demand compliance and issue ultimatums." Her sister's words had merit.

Irish Jewel

BY

Julie Ann James

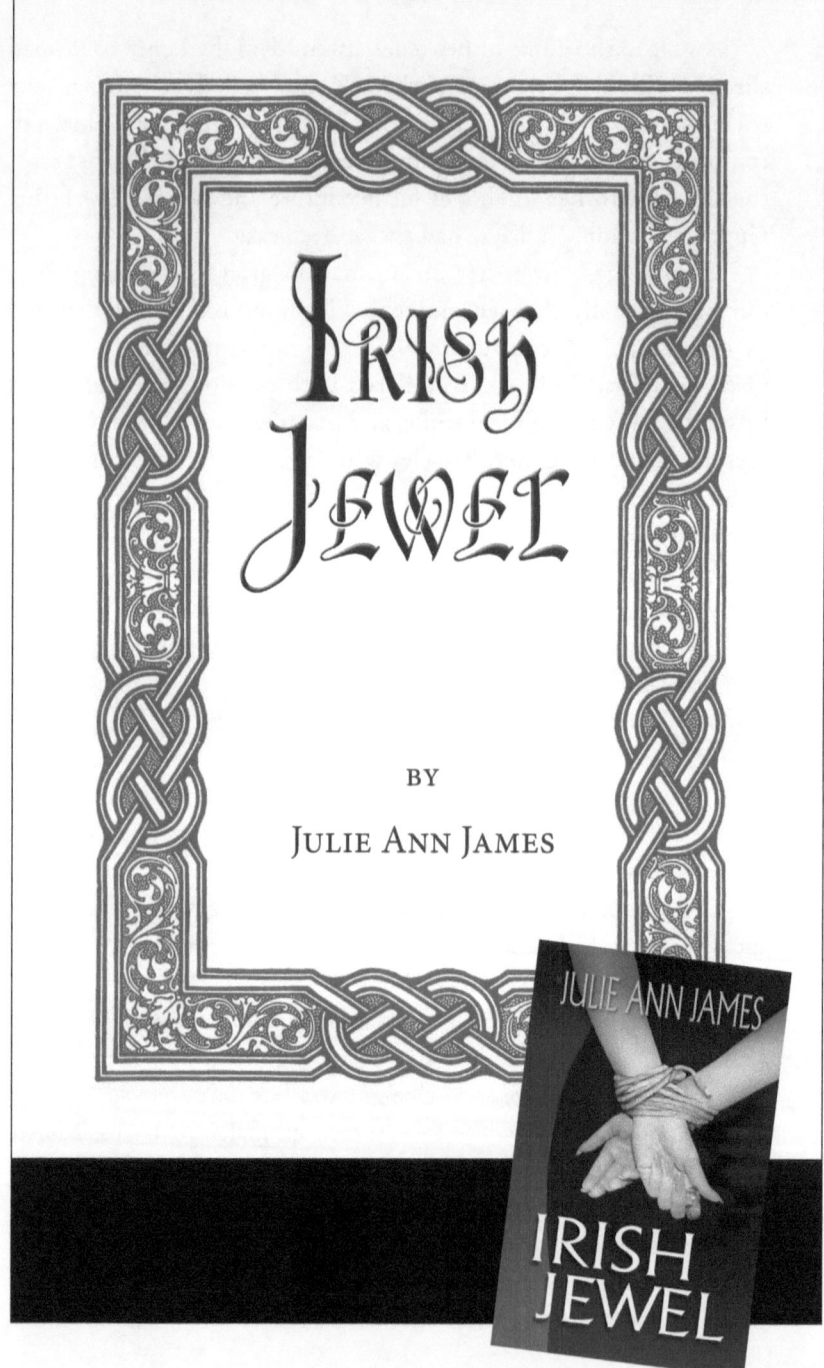

CHAPTER ONE

T HE CAPTAIN'S DEEP MONOTONE VOICE INTERRUPTED the restless sleep of some 120 passengers to prepare them for touchdown. They were about 20 minutes outside the Dublin airport at the end of a smooth but long flight, something that Amy Reid was still getting used to since her engagement to the love of her life, an Irishman, Michael Cambridge. They had met two years earlier as seatmates on a flight out of Dublin to her hometown of Sarasota, Florida.

Since then, they had been inseparable, other than the exasperating fact they lived across the pond from one another, which put an unexpected spin on the term, "long distance relationship." Last summer, his proposal was sweet and romantic. Following a shared meal, he offered her an after-dinner mint, and hidden inside the wrapper, a princess-cut diamond ring, a whopping three-carats! His family is in the jewelry business. How lucky can a girl be to wear on her left hand what are literally the family jewels?

It was hard to believe that their wedding would take place in ten days after months of planning, choosing the perfect dress, and brilliantly persuading her entire family to make the trip to Ireland. Now that most of the details had fallen into place, she felt as though she had conquered all. A March wedding in

Ireland—inside a castle—was a dream come true for any girl.

The seatbelt sign turned off, giving passengers permission to move about the cabin. Amy rifled through her purse making certain all her belongings were in order, pulled her carry-on out from the overstuffed compartment, and took her place in the crowded aisle.

The flight attendants thanked the passengers for flying Aer Lingus and provided concise directions on how to get from the gate to the baggage claim. Amy couldn't care less what they were talking about, as her mind was in an entirely different place. She couldn't believe she was going to marry someone she considered to be her soulmate. As corny as that sounded, she made sure complete strangers were aware that she was about to marry a "Cambridge."

The Cambridges were known for their generosity, as they donated to charitable organizations throughout the country. They hosted elaborate parties at their estate located just outside County Clare—all on behalf of the miracle of medical research for so many causes. This made a lasting impression on Amy and was one of the many traits she admired about Michael. The Cambridge donations made a huge difference in many deserving lives. The family's name and pictures were plastered in the newspaper quite often, but for the greater good, which was refreshing to say the least.

Michael wasn't able to pick her up from the airport due to a work thing, so she was prepared to hail a cab to take her to their temporary flat in the city. It felt so good to be back in Ireland, where the Celtic history overflowed in each charming town. It wasn't unusual that one of their endearing people would offer a

30-minute dissertation of that history in response to one simple question.

To her pleasant surprise, a limo waited for her arrival outside the airport doors—Michael's doing no doubt. The driver, in a sleek black suit and top hat, rescued her from her heavy bags and opened the door with a gracious nod and smile.

"Thank you so much—this is great. I can't believe Michael did this for me. Wait, what am I talking about? Of course, he did this—he's Michael. You will have to forgive me, driver. I often talk to myself, so pay no attention to me. I am just so very excited to be getting married in ten days—count them, ten days—in Ireland for that matter." Amy held up her freshly manicured hands to give the visual of ten days as she slid into the back seat.

"So I have heard, Miss Reid. That rumor has been spreading all around town. Believe me, everyone knows of your upcoming wedding. The Cambridges might just as well be royalty." His eyes sparkled directly at hers, and then he closed the door.

"I am going to be a bride, Michael's bride." She giggled and danced her feet on the floorboard of the moving limo.

Amy settled back into the plush leather seat and pulled out her overstuffed wedding planner, skimming the pages for the final "to dos" before the "I dos" actually took place. Of course, her newly launched ad agency back in Sarasota had been somewhat difficult to leave behind and was always on her mind. But she had great confidence in her staff. They should be able to hold down the fort in her absence.

Lorenzo's Rules:

LORD OF THE NINTH UNDERWORLD

BY

Stewart Stearns

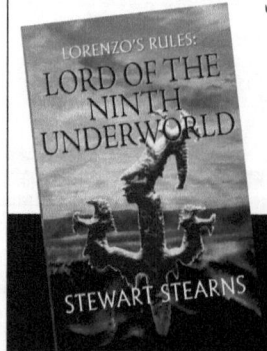

DAY ONE

Gregorian Date: *Monday, 13 August*
Tzol'kin Dare: *4 Acauc*
A day of transformation

CHAPTER 1

It was still dark when Lorenzo Rojas Batz boarded the brightly painted Blue Bird bus with the word "Flores" boldly painted on the side. Although it was late 1970's there were no formal time schedules for any of the *camionetas,* Lorenzo was relatively certain that this bus was destined to leave at around 6:00 AM for Guatemala City, or *Guate,* the more common name. It always did. Lorenzo could never afford a watch, but he was also relatively certain that it was currently around 5 AM. By boarding now, he could have his pick of rows of seats.

He carefully chose a row that would be neither too close to the driver nor too close to the back of the bus. If the bus careened off the steep roads because the driver needed to demonstrate his *machismo* at the expense of his passengers, Lorenzo wanted to be seated in a neutral spot — a place where he would neither fly out of the front window nor be crushed by the weight of items being propelled out of the back of the bus.

Each time Lorenzo made this long trip (four hours one way; eight hours, there and back); he promised it would be his last. The truth was that he had never enjoyed traveling to Guate. Even as a child, he was nauseated by the foul smell of diesel fumes that polluted the capitol city, but a trip there always made him appreciate the cool clean mountain air of the Western Guatemalan Highlands or *Altiplano* and his beloved city of La Paz. By boarding early, he had the opportunity to sit quietly and enjoy the almost-chilly morning, the dark, and the silence. Too soon, other passengers would be packing their bodies into the bus so tightly that it would be hard to breathe, and he would be forced to share his carefully chosen seat with at least two other adults, several children and often some live chickens and pigs.

Lorenzo was neither quite asleep nor quite awake when the sound of a police siren made him jump. He could probably count on one hand the number of times he had heard a police siren in La Paz, and none of those times were before the sun had risen.

As the longstanding indigenous mayor or *Alcalde Indígena*, he paid close attention to disasters such as fires, floods or murders — events that could generate the use of a siren — because it was ultimately his job to try to help the affected families, even though he had no financial or governmental resources at his disposal.

Lorenzo's authority came from the appointment he received from an assembly of local Maya Ki'iche elders. At times, the departmental government recognized his authority, and at times they did not. Although concerned about the nature of this emergency, Lorenzo settled back into his reverie. Today would be a one-day trip. He should be home at dusk to resume his duties. Whatever had caused the police to break this morning's peaceful silence with the shrill siren would be there tomorrow.

Lorenzo was about to slip back into semi-consciousness when the flicker of interior bus lights made him sit up straight. The bus driver and his assistant or *ayudante* were getting the bus ready for departure. "*¡Buenas días!*" the driver shouted to anyone within earshot as he sat down in the driver's seat colorfully surrounded with pompoms and a *retrato* of La Virgen de Guadelupe.

"*¡Buenas!*" shouted Lorenzo, returning the obligatory pleasantry.

Within a few moments, passengers started boarding. There were no tickets, no receipts, no refunds, and U.S. dollars were accepted since one quetzal equaled one dollar exactly, as it had for many years. The ayudante went from person to person to collect the two *quetzales* and fifty *centavo* fare to Guate. Lorenzo always marveled at these young men's ability to remember each passenger, charge them accordingly, and return exact change to each traveler even though they may not have it at the time of purchase.

For as many years as he had been the indigenous mayor of the many citizens of La Paz and its surrounding communities, he might expect that he would know absolutely everyone on the bus. But today he recognized only a few faces. This either attested to the growth that La Paz was undergoing or his fear that aging was gradually damaging his memory. Since he couldn't do anything about either, he settled back into his seat.

Memoirs

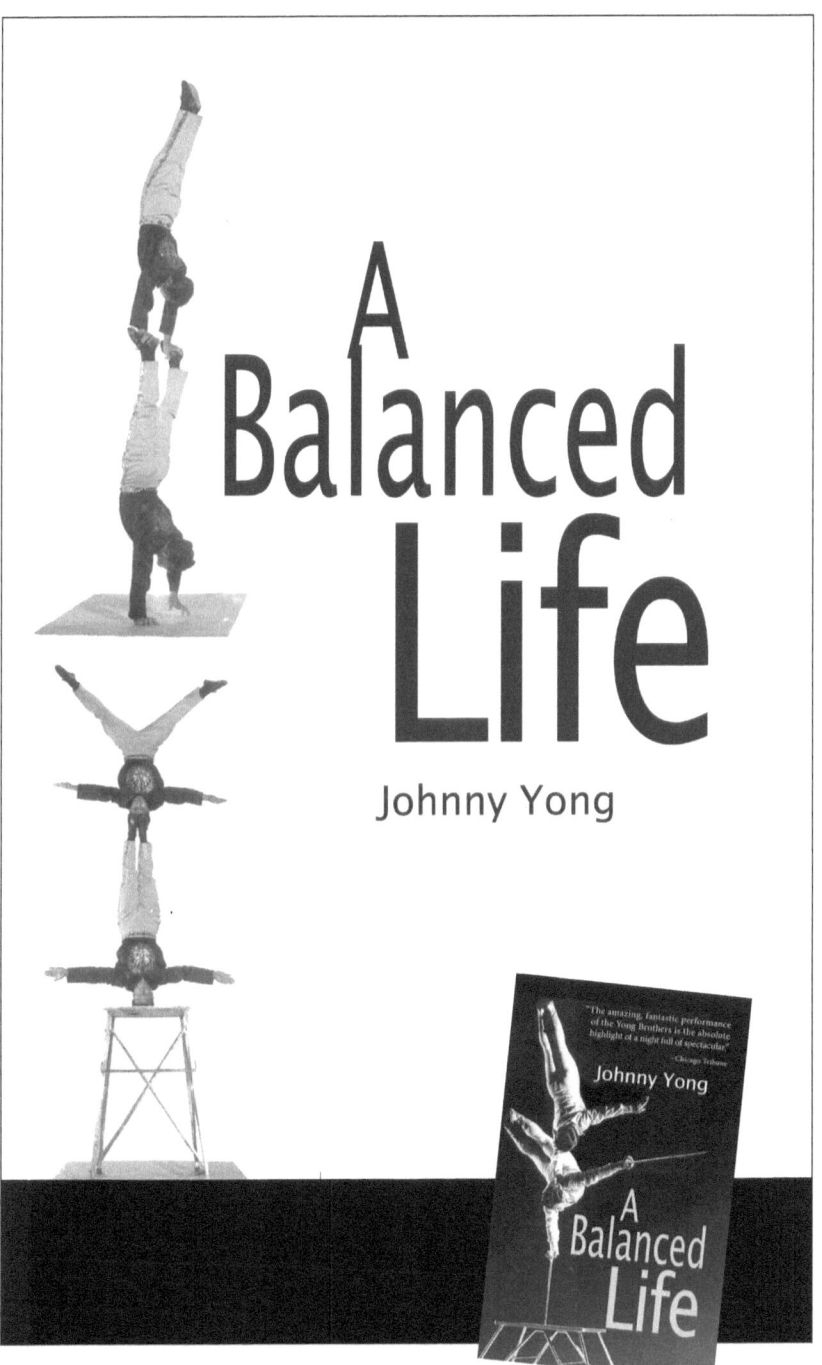

A Balanced Life

Johnny Yong

Acknowledgement

First and foremost, I want to acknowledge my great debt to Robert Van Praag who assisted me in putting my fond memories into words. Robert's tremendous writing skills enabled me to share the traveling experiences of *The Yong Brothers*. During the time we shared working on this book, Robert and I enjoyed our company together.

We forged a friendship that will endure for many years to come...Johnny Yong.

Prologue

"Are you really sure that a floor can't also be a ceiling?"

~M.C. Escher~

ADULTS OFTEN RECALL, OR POSSIBLY ASSUME SINCE they do the same thing, the many times that as children adults would look down at them (specifically the aunt who not only pinched your cheek but liked to mush it like silly putty) and ask in their imitation of a child's giddy voice their favorite opening sentence to a child who can't even tie their shoe laces yet, "So, what do *you* want to be when you grow up?"

As the child matures from four, five, to even six the answers go from cowboy, fireman, policeman, and then that wonderful time when their mothers get teary eyed as they say doctor.

Then there is the time that the child's imagination really goes wild after seeing a comic book, a parade, or talking with friends and announces to the world he wants to be in the *circus*! There is not a smile larger in the world than the time that the child screams the phrase he wants to be in the circus to a room full of laughing adults.

Then the laughter stops, the child's fantasies of trapezes, lions, and clowns fade yet somewhere in the back of his mind there is always that dream of, *"Wow, the circus!"*

No one ever stooped down to me (although my cheek is still bruised) and asked me, "What do you want to be when you grow up?"

My life was planned before I was even born.

The only thing that is unfortunate is that I cannot come up with a better phrase than "thank you." Of course, the appropriate question would be more akin to, "Why was I born so lucky?"

The dream that enters little kids minds and stays in the subconscious of all adults who manage to retain the gift of a child's innocence and fantasy for me was not then, nor throughout my life, a dream. More like a wish come true that I didn't even know I wished for.

What do I want to be when I grow up? The same thing I wanted when I was five, six, twenty, and forty…

…to be in the circus.

What *was* I when I grew up? *The same thing I was* when I was five, six, twenty, and forty…

…in the circus.

To children and adults I say dreams not only can, but do come true because dreams are only goals waiting for action.

My secret: A Balanced Life.

"It is possible to read upside down; it all depends upon how you see the world."

~Johnny Yong~

Chapter One

"Magic is believing in yourself, if you can do that,
you can make anything happen."

~Johann Wolfgang von Goethe~

I BEGIN MY STORY WITH A COMPLETE TRUTH. One that many will not accept. Some because they do not believe it is possible. A lot because they do not want to face what they themselves did not possess.

I had a happy childhood.

And, much to the dismay of my mother's neighboring countryman Sigmund Freud, I loved both of my parents very much and I do not have any latent mother issues that need to be resolved.

Although I was blessed with a happy childhood, the one thing that to this day I cannot understand is that after traveling most of the world I have not found a single country who celebrates May 8, 1935 as a national holiday. I firmly believe it should be. It is my birthday.

If you can now accept that I am not lying in regards to my happy childhood, the next fact might make you again question your belief in me. I was born in Germany. Yes, in 1935; and I am being so bold as to tell you that I had a happy childhood; not regardless of the environment I was born into, but in spite of it.

My credibility gets tested further. I do not have any horror stories of the War. For me, it was entertaining. *No*, not as you think. Do not be ready to toss me aside as a Nazi and all that is associated with that word.

It was entertaining because I was, I am, an entertainer. One who was born into a horrible time and place where the concept of entertainment seems at the best, banal. At the worst, a sin. In many cases, a mortal sin.

I was a child; I lived in Germany throughout World War II. I am thankful that the atrocities that occurred during those years did not directly affect me. And, as distasteful as it might sound, all thoughts of the Third Reich as you view them need to be kept separate from my story, my life.

Unbeknownst to me, I learned something at this early stage of my life, a time when a child exists without complete understanding, which not only stayed within me but became the core basis for who I am. A child might not be a part (be that physically or shielded) of a war any more than a child might not be a part of a depression (ibid) but the effect it leaves upon them is a determinate part of their personality throughout their entire life

My father was born in China into a renowned family of acrobatic performers. On their own, they truly are legendary. My father traveled (performed) throughout the world and before he made his way to Germany was a feature act in the American vaudeville circuit where he performed with many of the greats including the master Al Jolson.

the Lady and the Sharks

Eugenie Clark

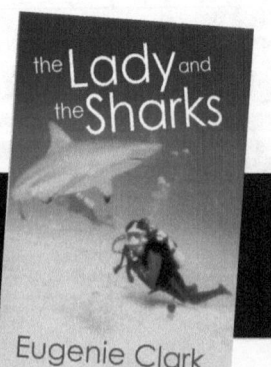

1 Discovering a Watery Eden

THE WEST COAST OF FLORIDA is edged by a series of sandy keys, with bays between them and the mainland, and the Gulf of Mexico on their outer sides. Where man has not cleared the bay shoreline, it is dense with mangrove trees whose overhanging branches and roots, reaching into the water, provide protective cover and substrate for the rich marine and estuarine life. If you look at a map of Florida, two huge drainages stand out on the west coast, Tampa Bay and Charlotte Harbor. From these the rains and tides wash abundant nutrients into the Gulf. Only Charlotte Harbor, of the large estuaries in this country on the Gulf of Mexico and Atlantic Coast south of

Cape Cod, is still virtually unpolluted. Deep Boca Grande Pass, the entrance to Charlotte Harbor, is the most famous place in the world for tarpon fishing and large hammerhead sharks—a real challenge in bringing your tarpon boatside in one piece. Northwest of Boca Grande, Charlotte Harbor leads into Gasparilla Sound, then narrows to a slit which opens into Lemon Bay. Big and Little Gasparilla islands are said to be the place in which the pirate Gasparilla buried his treasure.

My introduction to the west coast of Florida was in 1954 after I accepted an invitation from Anne and William H. Vanderbilt to give a lecture in Englewood, Florida. Mrs. Vanderbilt had read my book *Lady with a Spear* and talked her husband into reading it. Their ten-year-old son, Bill Jr., had a bedroom full of aquariums, as I did at his age, and his parents had become fascinated with their son's hobby. Their estate stretched across Manasota Key, from Lemon Bay to the Gulf of Mexico. Bill Jr. and his school chums, like all children living near the water, explored the shore and brought home all kinds of strange sea life they found in shallow water or washed up on the beach. But many of these items they couldn't identify; a few mystified them even after they consulted books, teachers, and the local fishermen. There was no marine biologist in the area.

William and his brother, Alfred Gwynne Vanderbilt, had bought a 36,000-acre tract of land near the fishing village of Placida, southeast of Englewood, extending onto the Cape Haze peninsula. They had started raising Santa Gertrudis cattle at their newly formed 2V Ranch and were developing land along the miles of waterfront property in this beautiful, isolated, semitropical country. Alfred Vanderbilt had also decided to build a house in their Cape Haze development, where his family could enjoy the beaches, boating, and fishing and where, in his private plane, he could easily hop over to see his horses when they ran at Hialeah.

My evening talk was given in the Englewood public school and was open to the public. There were many children and commercial fishermen with their families. Some stood in the doorways to hear what I thought would have limited appeal— a lecture on Red Sea fishes. I learned from the comments as I lectured that for almost every unusual fish I mentioned or showed on colored slides, a similar fish had been seen at Englewood; giant sting rays, mantas, guitarfish, scorpion fish, electric rays, nurse, hammerhead, tiger sharks, and many other spectacular fish were known also to the local fishermen, who wanted to find out more about them in the long question/answer session after the lecture.

My own interest in sea life had begun when I was in elementary school in New York. My American father died when I was a baby, and my Japanese-born mother was working at the cigar and newspaper stand in the lobby of the Downtown Athletic Club. On Saturdays, while she worked, she left me nearby in the old New York Aquarium at Battery Park, where I spent many hours watching the fishes. Afterward we usually went to eat at a charming little Japanese restaurant, Fuji, and gradually became good friends with the owner and cook, Masatomo Nobu, who later became my stepfather. I was brought up on the Japanese side of my family, but no one, except anthropologists who are quick to spot my Mongolian eyefold, ever thinks I'm part Japanese.

I knew more about produce from the sea than any of my schoolmates, and my reports in school, from kindergarten on, amused and shocked my classmates and teachers. I told them how we ate with chopsticks, had rice and seaweed for breakfast, raw fish, octopus, and sea urchin eggs for supper, and cakes made from sharks. I was the only student of Japanese ancestry in the schools where I grew up, in Woodside, Long Island.

Nobusan often visited my family (Grandma Yuriko, Uncle Boya, and Mama) and always brought us some special Japanese delicacies from his restaurant. He already seemed part of the family when he became my stepfather, at the time I graduated from Hunter College. I had majored in zoology. Since my first visits to the Aquarium at Battery Park, I had wanted to be an ichthyologist. Graduate courses at the University of Michigan, Columbia University, Woods Hole, Scripps Institute of Oceanography, and at New York University, where I got my master's and doctorate degrees, prepared me for scholarships that took me to various parts of the world to study fishes. I had visited marine laboratories in many countries, and in my book I described a small, isolated marine biological laboratory in the little fishing town of Ghardaqa, on the Egyptian coast of the Red Sea, where I had studied fishes for a year as a Fulbright Research Scholar in 1951.

I never dreamed I would have the opportunity to start a laboratory from scratch myself, but later on the evening of my lecture in Englewood I learned that the Vanderbilts had invited me to Florida for just this reason. They felt the stimulating, strong interest and importance of marine life in their part of Florida, and wanted to help develop this interest in some worthwhile way. Bill Vanderbilt told me, "It's Anne's idea. She thinks it would be just great if we had a marine laboratory here, something like the one you described in your book. The rest of us are all for it, too. What do you think? Is this a suitable place for that kind of research? Would you consider starting a marine laboratory and being the director?"

It was an exciting offer—an opportunity to study fishes and other marine life and to create a laboratory. The west coast of Florida was quite different from the tropical coral reef areas where I had done most of my research. There were many basic things I would have to learn about the less clear waters around a major estuary. And there were no strings attached, no contract; I didn't have to make any promises, just "Start a place here where people can learn more about the sea" was all the Vanderbilts asked of me.

I knew there were no marine biological laboratories in this part of Florida. In the 1930s, the New York Aquarium had had a small research station some miles south on Palmetto Key. In my studies I had often referred to the valuable scientific publications of Director Charles M. Breder Jr. and other scientists who had studied how tarpon got into fresh water, the mouth-breeding habits of poisonous catfish, the floating leaf mimicry of baby spadefish, and other fascinating phenomena of sea creatures. This series of scientific studies seemed to be just the start of an endless amount of research that could be done on the fertile, complex part of the sea in the estuaries and on the wide, rich continental shelf in this part of the west coast of Florida.

Unfortunately, this kind of basic research does not often get the support that applied research can get. The Palmetto Key Laboratory closed after a few years for lack of funds. Many a scientist has had to leave the freedom, creativity, and exciting experimental studies in basic research for restricted research in an industrial or other "practical" laboratory in order to support a growing family. It is hard for many people to understand the basic scientist's desire to learn the answer to a question just for the sake of new knowledge.

FLORENCE

LOVE ◉ ART ◉ ARTISTS
FRAGMENTS OF MY LIFE

by Giuliana

A FEBRUARY MORNING IN GREENWICH

I was sitting in my beautiful, spacious dining room like a guest in my own house. Only on a few occasions has the room been opened to guests to brighten our social life in Greenwich. I was having my morning espresso in the manner that a lady would have her *petit déjeuner,* pretending maids were in the kitchen cleaning up the dishes. Contrary to most European women who like to spend most of their time in the kitchen even when they entertain, I prefer to be far away from pots and pans and cooking smells which distract my mind.

In our early years of marriage, we did not have a dining room. In New York, our dining room was the entrance hall where we put a table for our meals, and at other times the kitchen was used as a dinette. When we moved to this house in Greenwich, we began living more graciously. Having experienced life without a dining room, I did not take for granted what comfort meant to us in our mature years, and I enjoyed our life style in Greenwich.

Sitting at the end of our long cherry table on a cold February morning, I waited for David to get up. From my chair, I looked out of my beautiful Tudor windows at the garden where Sam, our cat, lay buried, and watched the branches of the trees slowly moving in the winter breeze.

As I was staring at the view, the trees suddenly became people standing there looking at me. It was as if a silent conversation had been conjured up by my imagination from a desire to be with others, a subconscious illusion to extend myself beyond the walls which were keeping me warm.

Inside my charming château, built sixty years ago, I visualized those Italian immigrants who worked to make a living in this community of English-Protestant residents. I admired my countrymen's labor of more than half a century ago and the beauty of our stone house that they so harmoniously constructed.

The dining room furniture was mostly English pieces in the Queen Anne style and had belonged to my mother-in-law. The other pieces were a mixture of French and Spanish. The large oriental carpet beneath the table warmed my bare feet, and from the ceiling a Waterford crystal chandelier illuminated the dark room. A gold mirror on the opposite wall reflected Redmore's painting of English sailing ships which hung above the fireplace behind me. The walls were covered with a Chinese print, depicting flying birds, small peach branches, and pink flowers on a background of dark cobalt. The centerpiece on the table was a bouquet of silk flowers; a gift from one of my friends, it reminded me of her pretty face and delicate hands. Some old pieces of rococo silver added to the atmosphere of subdued elegance.

The three dining room doors controlled traffic during our large parties. One led to the kitchen; another, a glass door framed with dark brown wooden panels, was across from the front entrance door; and the third, on the opposite side, opened to the back garden. From where I sat, the glass door amplified my vision, showing the hall outside as well as the interior castle:* my soul-searching for God.

I was drinking my coffee and looking at the Sunday edition of the *New York Times*. I began to eliminate section after section of the paper in order to read the most interesting news. I glanced at the volume of newspaper scattered on the table, wondering about the wasteful economy where everything is an example of grandiosity.

I read about the Contra White House scandal and the "Baby M" case (the surrogate mother fighting to adopt the child she conceived)

---

* *St. Teresa of Avila. "The Collected Works of St. Teresa of Avila" V.II. Translated by Kieran Kavonaugh y Rodriguez. (Washington, D. C. ICS Pub., 1980), p. 263*

when suddenly a telephone call shook the silent monastery.

"Yes," I answered.

A pleasant voice said, "Giuliana?"

"Nelson? Is that you?" My soprano voice rose in pitch revealing my happy emotion, but soon scaled down after he gave me the news.

"Nerina Simi died last night. Please tell David." He spoke in haste, abruptly ending the call and leaving me cold.

For a moment I was motionless, thinking of Nelson who called from Florence, Italy where he worked as secretary to the artist Pietro Annigoni and paints Italian landscapes. A good friend of David's, Nelson was a bachelor whose family lived in Waterford, Connecticut. His mother, a noble Italian lady, had married an American. Although I had not seen Nelson for many years, I was fond of his gentle manner and storytelling power which was enhanced by his funny Italian accent.

I returned to my paper that was spread all over the table, but I remained still. The news of the death was taking effect on me; I felt cold. I realized the heat was still off, and I got up to turn up the thermostat. Outside everything was tapestried with clean snow. Solitude and peace surrounded me.

Ever since I was a young girl, coping with death had been my innermost battle. I saw my father-in-law die from cancer, and my mother-in-law succumbed to the same illness after five years of suffering. I began to accept what I could not change: Giuliana had matured late. Indeed I changed at the realization of what aging means.

From my religious upbringing, death was always present in my mind, but it was my sensitive nature that fought the human reality. I even disliked natural events, such as the birth of a baby, which I saw as a painful and ugly experience. Was I young and immature with an aesthetic sensibility?

Suddenly a baritone voice called. In what language was he addressing me? Usually it was a combination of American-Italian mixed with either French or Spanish. We are two polyglots using our tongues to converse in different languages, as well as to taste the delicate food of those nations.

"*Oh, oh.... omelette á la florentine*," he said, discovering his plate in the oven.

The so called lady guest got up to serve *Il caro nome David.*
Caro nome che il cor festi palpitar. . . . (Dear name, my heart enshrines...)
Verdi Rigoletto

The Conversation
by David

NERINA AND FILADELFO SIMI
ARTISTS IN FLORENCE

David was sitting at the kitchen table looking outside at the birds eating from different feeders. Cardinals, sparrows, finches, woodpeckers, and blue jays were coming and going, while a fat quail was calmly pecking a few seeds on the ground. There were peeled sunflower seeds in the satellite, another kind of seed in the cylindrical feeder and a mixture of seeds in the cover dish. Hanging above was a seed bell and a ball of suet, a balanced diet for a long, cold winter in Greenwich.

A squirrel was maneuvering quickly to grasp some pieces of bread in the snow. David got up furiously and opened the glass door to chase him away. Squirrels were his enemies. They damaged his garden by eating his strawberries, figs and corn after he had worked for hours on hot summer days.

It was no longer snowing when I finally told him about Nelson's call. David had already finished his breakfast, but was still sitting in front of his empty plate. He didn't say anything, not a word. I left the kitchen to water the plants in the living room, and when I returned he asked me about the funeral arrangements. "The Italian radio will broadcast the news of her death, and the religious service will take place on the next day." I informed him.

Memoirs of the Good Ole Days

Dorothy Klein Johnson

Compiled by Jean Johnson Moenning
and Susan Moenning Janz

The Family

Our parents were George Jacob Klein and Osa Ives Henderson. Dad was born April 13, 1879, and died December 13, 1943. His parents were Jacob Klein and Dora Bohne. They came from Germany by boat. Grandma's first job was working for a family doing cooking and cleaning.

Mother was born April 13, 1884, and died April 15, 1952. Her parents were Thomas L. Henderson and Sarah Newcomb. Their home was on the River Road, now named Henderson Road. As far as I know, she was born there. We all loved to go to Grandpa Henderson's on Sunday afternoon. Grandma died when I was quite young. Therefore, I don't remember her well.

When Dad was quite young, Grandma and Grandpa moved to Vincennes, where the Germans were settling. They moved there from Trenton, Illinois.

Grandpa built a small brick home where Dad's home place is located on South Sixth Street Road. Later they added to the house and made it into the home it is today.

The house had an upstairs, but we never went up there. Their main room was always warm in the winter. There was an old wooden kitchen table and sideboard with a mirror across the back, and three drawers in the front. Grandma's cookies were here, and Grandpa's wine bottle was in the closet. This room holds a lot of memories.

The front room was a very special guest room for people who called and said they were coming. It had a beautiful fireplace made of marble with pretty porcelain figurines on

Our New House

Mother and Dad moved into this old house when they were married. I think this is Uncle Chester with Mother and Dad's dog. Uncle Chester was Mother's brother. I do not remember this during the 1913 flood. Mother said everyone worked so hard getting furniture up on tables and moving things out so the water wouldn't get to them.

Figure 17 – Our Old House, Uncle Chester

The men took the cows and mules to Uncle Otto's farm, as his ground was higher. The balance of the livestock was taken to Dad's place, called the Deckard place.

Mother said she heard the roar of the water coming from

the Wabash and knew the levee had broken. She said I was looking out the window watching for Uncle Otto, as he was coming to get us in the spring wagon and we were going to their house.

She was doing last minute little jobs, but grabbed me up along with the three older boys as Uncle Otto came in. We had to hurry to get ahead of the water. Before we came to the railroad crossing going to Uncle Otto's house, the muddy water was beginning to cover the road.

1913 Flood Made the Washout a Swimming Hole

Figure 19 – 1913 Flood, Old Sow Had Babies

This is Grandma Klein on the porch of their house and also the barn.

Figure 20 – 1913 Flood

When the water was built up against the railroad tracks, it came with such force that the railroad track was broken. The large washout below our house was one break. This washout was later used as the boys' swimming hole. I think it is still there, but is used now by the Skeet Club. We always picked nice blackberries around it.

After the water receded, there was a lot of work to do, so much cleaning and livestock to be brought back. Some of mother's furniture was usable; other pieces weren't. She used her dining room

Meinord Pitched

table until she left the old house. It was in the water, in the house, floating around with other pieces. This table was oak and extended across our new dining room. It was full length, and used many times for family dinners, butchering and threshing.

Mother and Dad made do with the old house until they recovered from the flood. After some time they began to think of building a new house. Dad and Mother began to make plans.

Paul and Meinord

A Mr. Ed Frieze, a friend of Dad's from Germany, was a bricklayer by trade. He had built his own home (it still stands on Twelfth and Busseron). Dad thought a brick house would be nice and wanted Mr. Frieze to lay the brick.

Dad wanted the old house moved out of the way and the new one put in its place. He loved the old cottonwood and elm trees that were in the yard.

At that time, there wasn't electricity any place but in town. He talked to Public Service of Indiana about getting it down South Sixth Street Road. They told him there had to be at least four families who would take it before they would consider putting it in. Those who did decide would pay for the poles at a price of fifty dollars each.

Dad talked to Grandpa Klein (Jacob), Uncle Jack (J.W.), and Mr. J. B. E. La Plante and asked if they were interested.

There was a lot of red tape and a long wait, but soon electricity was on its way.

Mr. La Plante was president of either the local bank or a financial firm. They lived on La Plante Hill. He and his wife had two sons. They drove a big black car, and always dressed so nice. We always thought he was real nice, because he let us take our sleds and slide down his big hill in the winter.

Self Help

The EMPOWERING of YOU
PART ONE OF A TRILOGY !!!
T. Donald Burns

The **MYTH** of Employee Burnout

What it is.
Why it happens.
What to do about it.

MATT HELLER

NORMAN L. QUANTZ, MA

It's All About Power and Control

Why Marriages Fall Apart and What it Takes to Put Them Back Together Again

A **Language** of the **Heart**
THERAPY STORIES THAT HEAL

2ND EDITION

D. FRANKLIN SCHULTZ, PhD

The
MYTH
of
Employee Burnout

What it is.
Why it happens.
What to do about it.

MATT HELLER

Chapter 1
My Introduction to Burnout

I first experienced employee burnout in 1991. I was a Group Leader at Canobie Lake Park in Salem, New Hampshire, and was responsible for the performance and morale of 50+ employees in the Rides department. It was my third season at the park, and I couldn't believe that I had found such a cool summer job.

As late July rolled around, I noticed a palpable change in the excitement and enthusiasm of my staff. Gone were the smiles and cheery dispositions, now being replaced by sluggish saunters and one-word answers.

I wondered what had happened until a veteran of the amusement park business informed me that this was just a typical case of midseason burnout, and that it happened every year. He said the heat, dealing with guests, and the long hours eventually take their toll on the employees. If that was true, I wondered why I had not noticed this during my first two summers at the park. Of course I knew there were people who didn't seem to like their jobs, but I figured that was the case anywhere you went, and I didn't associate it with a particular time of year. I also didn't know it was because of something called burnout.

I think the other reason I was pleasantly oblivious to it was that I wasn't in a leadership role those first two seasons, and my job didn't center around trying to get other people to live up to the park's high standards and to entertain our guests day in and day out. I only had to worry about myself. Now I was privy to all the ups and downs of employee morale, and in fact, was responsible for it.

Fast forward to 2009. My career had taken me from New Hampshire to Minnesota, Minnesota to Connecticut, and Connecticut to Florida—all in the pursuit of going as far as I possibly could in the amusement park business. I had been bitten by the "business of fun" bug and wasn't looking for a cure. What I WAS still looking for a cure for, though, was employee burnout.

It seemed like no matter what company I worked for, large or small, they all struggled with employee burnout. Even outside of the attractions business, people were complaining about the fact that employees would start off enthused and eager to please and then somewhere along the line would turn sour and hard to handle. The funny thing is, we knew it was coming so we planned for ways to overcome it. We tried incentive programs and giveaways and pizza parties, but ultimately burnout still happened. We were stumped.

And it seemed to be a growing problem. As a member of the IAAPA (International Association of Amusement Parks and Attractions) Human Resources Committee, I got to talk to many others around the industry about what they were going through with their employees. Over and over again, people asked, "Do you have any ideas on how to keep employees motivated throughout the season? The middle of the season burnout is killing us."

So what's the big deal? Why are so many people worried about this burnout thing? Because burned-out employees are not productive employees. Because unmotivated employees can be rude and tough to deal with. And most importantly, because your employees ARE your bottom line. Your employees, and the way they behave, impact:

- Revenue
- Profit
- Sales
- Safety
- Guest Service
- Employee Relations
- Recruiting
- Marketing

And the list goes on. Everything that you work for and everything that you measure is impacted by your employees. If they burn out, they directly impact all of these factors. This could be the difference between your success and failure as a business.

I want you to be successful. So I went on a quest to uncover the truth about burnout. Let's see what I found...

Chapter 2
My Quest

One of my favorite movies is National Lampoon's Vacation, and at one point our hero Clark Griswold tells his family that they are no longer on vacation, they are now on "A quest. A quest for fun." I decided it was time for me to go on a quest to really find out what was going on with this burnout thing so we could finally have an answer for it. The results of that quest were quite interesting.

First, I had to examine the *phenomenon* of employee burnout. For it to be happening for so long, and for so many smart people to stymied by it, there had to be a disconnect somewhere. There had to be something that everyone was missing. My quest was to find out what that was.

I don't recall exactly when it hit me, but I remember thinking that almost every time I would talk to an industry colleague about employee burnout, the conversation would always take an inevitable turn. We would talk about how hot it got in the summer, the long hours employees were working, and the crazy guests we dealt with. Since this is what the industry pro had told me many years earlier, and we all agreed that these were the factors causing burnout, we all must be right, right?

SECTION ONE:

The Problem With Power and Control

CHAPTER 1

Troubled Marriages

*H*umans are hardwired for relationships.

Winners of the human race are those who excel in relationships. In other words, the purpose of the human race, if it could be simplified in one word, would be *relationship*. The importance of relationships in the human experience is undeniable. Endless evidence shows that the pursuit of relationship is overwhelmingly the most common human trait.

Relational freedom—personal wholeness that thrives in a relationship—is core to an exceptional life of deep satisfaction in any relationship.

In order to understand and excel at relationships, it is necessary to grasp the inner workings of each individual and how they use their *power and control*. The more you pursue what is true, whole, and beneficial about these components of power and control, and change on the basis of these truths, the more fulfilled and empowered you will be in your close relationships.

Relationships do not develop without the existence of power and control dynamics. *Healthy* relationships do not develop without the existence of *healthy* power and control dynamics.

Manipulation prevents healthy relationships from forming and, in fact, breaks down the very fabric of our being, thus preventing the joy of being in a close healthy relationship. This causes marriages to falter and fail and for many, it leaves them to muddle along in a disappointing relationship having lost all hope of achieving the harmony they dreamed of. So much abuse is being tolerated in marriage relationships, and some for no better reason than to be able to say they are faithfully committed to their marriage. Committed, but to what?

Consider how desperate people are to hang onto relationships that have long stalemated in the murk and mire of stagnation. How long does a woman have to cry herself to sleep while her husband is dead to the world, seemingly oblivious to the emotional chasm growing between them? Then, if and when he finally acknowledges there is a problem, he insists his wife accept him as he is because this is his personality—it is just how he was made. He justifies his behavior by blaming something while she continually adjusts her life to simply deal with it.

Humans are hard-wired for relationships.

How many live day and night with the suspicion and overwhelming evidence that they are not loved? How many broken hearts start the day's work trying to forget the arguments of the night before? And what about those who believe they have a good relationship because no one is getting hit or physically harmed? Can passivity contribute to angst in the other partner? How many people go about their day with a cheerful attitude and smiling face when inside they are falling apart? How many holes in the walls and doors are covered up by striking posters or beautiful artwork while hiding the evidence of the violent outbursts?

You have a reason for reading today. If any of this has piqued your interest, this book is for you. The insights in this book have been taken from many years of success and failure observed in working with clients and students to develop deep, wholesome relationships. It could be just what you need to save your relationship.

So why, in all the books and articles written, all the studies undertaken, all the conclusions drawn, and all the experiments completed do we as humans continue to fail at such a rapid rate in the very activity we are hardwired to pursue? It is certainly not for lack of trying!

In the mid-1980s, I first became aware of the idea that *power and control* issues were connected with abuse in relationships. This phrase seemed to provide a framework of understanding that clarified the common issues in those difficult, seemingly irresolvable cases in my counseling practice.

I returned time and time again to the theme of building healthy power and control in a relationship, especially the close ones that people cherish. By reflecting on my own marriage and family struggles and successes, and those heart-wrenching stories from my counseling clients and students, it became obvious that a healthy relationship was closely tied to wholesome power and control. Not equal power but using power for good.

What has troubled me as a relationship therapist is how easily clients settle for a mere hint of fulfillment in a marriage rather than insisting on having a vibrant, close relationship. Or maybe we all should be encouraged! Perhaps the high divorce rate, in countries that allow

A Language of the Heart: Therapy Stories that Heal

2nd Edition

D. FRANKLIN SCHULTZ, PH.D.

Part One

A New Language

We have this story we tell ourselves, which is the story of our lives. We sometimes tell others parts of the story but mostly it is a personal narrative of who we think we are and what we think we are worth. As you read this section, begin to notice the language you use in this story of your life. Are the words you use kind and thoughtful or are they mean spirited? Do you treat yourself with respect or do you beat yourself up? Do you habitually call yourself names such as stupid, ugly, fat, skinny, clumsy, etc., or use more positive attributes? How do you speak to yourself when you make mistakes? Become especially mindful of the language you use in this narrative. Most of it is used by habit not because it is the Truth. You weren't born thinking bad things about yourself. You learned it. Begin to make an effort to change the language of your narrative to reflect kindness and patience, respect and understanding. Create a new habit of language in your narrative. This will take time and an effort to become conscious of your habits.

The exercises in this book should help you begin to change this narrative of your life. They are intended to help you change the way you think and talk to yourself about yourself and others. As the language of your story changes you will notice that you have a greater understanding and appreciation for your own (and others') experiences. You will notice you begin to treat yourself with the respect and dignity that you deserve. And you will notice you are much less reactive to the words and behaviors of those around you. You will begin to be more self-validated, relying on your own evaluation of yourself rather than what others think and say. You will also gain the ability to choose what you do next instead of just knee-jerk reacting emotionally. In other words, you will be more intentional. Finally, you will begin to recognize how important it is to have integrity, to say what you mean, mean what you say, and do what you say you are going to do, because this is how you will come to evaluate yourself.

What follows are "stories" about how we came to think about ourselves the way we do. They are arranged in a somewhat natural order. However, they may be read alone as complete sections. Clients report they find benefit in reading and re-reading sections as they need them. There are also exercises designed to help you understand the stories in a more personal way. The secret to your success with this book is using the exercises to change the language you use in the story of your life. My suggestion is that you read through the first half of the book entirely and then come back and re-read it, doing the exercises as you go. This is because some of the exercises should be done at the same time and you should know and be aware of them as you proceed.

A note of caution: Just reading the stories may give you some relief, but you will not gain much insight. It takes actually doing the exercises to receive the learning that each contains. There are unique nuances and layers of understanding for you only discovered by doing the exercises. A book such as this would never be able to describe all of these unique understandings. Do the exercises to gain the insight.

MAPS

From birth until about the age of eighteen is when we learn how we think about ourselves. It is when we learn how we think others think about us. It is when we learn how we think couples are supposed to be together, how we think lovers are supposed to be together, and how we think parents and children are supposed to be together. It is when we learn how to deal with anger and sadness, success and failure, joy, disappointment, fear, guilt and all the other significant emotions. What happens from zero to eighteen is that we create a template or map of how the world is supposed to work and how we are supposed to fit in it. Our map contains all of the ways we

The Empowering of You

PART ONE OF A TRILOGY III

T. Donald Burns

Being Overweight

Like a "prize fighter" you will need to "weigh in" Look at these as a start of a long awaited victory, not a battle.

WEIGH IN

Set a monthly cycle for checking your weight. The first of every month in the morning usually works best.

STAY AWAY FROM THE SCALE!

Here's why: during any nutritional change you can have "plateau days" where your weight won't change. However, you are going through a metabolic change and are probably losing inches. After about ten (10) days you will start to feel your clothes fitting a bit different! So don't worry about the scale!

Stick to it and remember to hydrate.

Check Yourself...
Before You Wreck Yourself!!

Take a hard look in the mirror. (Not a glance) Do you like what you see?

- Do you tire out prematurely?
- Do your clothes feel like they fit you correctly?
- Do you have low self esteem?
- Are you quick to judge people/things, snappy/close minded?
- Do you make excuses to get out of events/ activities?
- Do you fall asleep after eating, in places like the couch?
- Do you sleep for escape?
- Do you over-eat knowingly?
- Do you eat at improper times, like late at night?

These problems can be repaired!

Being Overweight is Correctable

Being overweight is a serious out; usually correctable problem. It can lead to a lot of health issues, such as; heart disease, diabetes, back problems and a whole host of others!

Your heart is a muscle like any other; it can only take so much strain. Don 't take it lightly, I never seen anyone want vascular bypass surgery!

A chiropractic physician once said if your carrying around fifty (50) or sixty (60) extra lbs. it's like carrying a bag of concrete; for no reason, not an easy task.

You will find with reasonable nutritional guide lines, easy general activities and cutting some stress out of your life most, if not all of this can be prevented.

Mind Set
Your Mind Set is Very Important!

- Are you feeling down?
- Lack self confidence?
- Alone frequently?
- Carry heavy sadness around?
- Usually the least optimistic of family or friends?

Not the way to go through life carrying this entire burden, like unnecessary baggage.

Don't let sadness and negativity weigh you down!

Negative Thoughts

Very wise men have told me, and take this one very seriously! "You don 't have a problem until you have a problem."

Mankind's worst enemy is fear of the unknown, or what I refer to as the "what if syndrome."

You can what if this and what if that you're self to death, worrying about trivial things or possible problem that nine (9) out often (10) time don't manifest into anything at all.

Inspiration

SIMPLY PRAY

Morning & Evening
Prayers for 31 Days

❖ ARCHIE BUIE ❖

A Spiritual Guidebook
for your Journey

JOY
in the
Morning

LINDA HETRICK

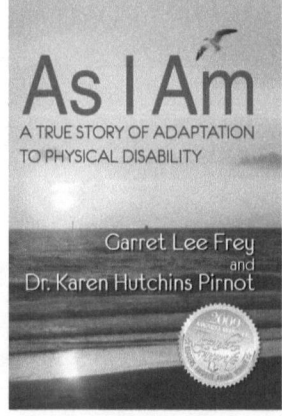

As I Am
A TRUE STORY OF ADAPTATION
TO PHYSICAL DISABILITY

Garret Lee Frey
and
Dr. Karen Hutchins Pirnot

"David, a man with a heart and a passion to connect with
God, hear from God and carry His voice to those in need."
—Vern Birkey

THE
OPTIONAL
ELEMENT

THE KEYS TO DEVELOPING
A SUCCESSFUL PRAYER LIFE

DR. DAVID SUTTON

Discover the Missing Elements That Will
Focus and Motivate Your Life in Prayer

SIMPLY PRAY

Morning & Evening
Prayers for 31 Days

ARCHIE BUIE

ME/YOU!

God, an unopened day, and I'm wondering how it will go.

I'm mostly concerned about my own comfort, my own happiness, my own success. Forgive me. Help me to shift my focus to what I can do for someone else— helping, really listening, encouraging, building up.

I'm mostly interested in what's good for me, and what I can get out of this day. Forgive me. Enable me to change my thinking so that I may do what pleases you, what you desire me to do.

I mostly want to put myself first, to satisfy my own wants, to get my own way. Forgive me. Help me to put you first, to deny myself, to bend down, to serve, to love without condition.

Today let my living bring you honor. In the name of your Son, who gave and gave and gave. Amen.

REPLENISH

God, I've spent much of the day giving
    my time,
        my attention,
           my energy,
               my effort,
                  my love.

People depend on me. There is much to do. My responsibilities never let up. Life demands more and more.

Now I feel empty, spent, and used up.

Help me! I open myself to you.

    Refresh my spirit.
    Replenish my energy.
    Restore my strength.

Through this night, make me new again, and grant me your peace. Amen.

Chapter One
Divine
Design!

"You made all the delicate, inner parts of my body and knit me together in my mother's womb."

Psalm 139:13,
(NLT)

A Story to Tell

With the choir quietly singing, "Just as I am, Without One Plea", at age twelve I approached the altar of Grace Methodist Church one hot, summer evening and committed my life to Christ and rose with all the zest and passion of a baby Christian. My new-born heart was on fire, thirsting to know more of God, and my prayer life was exploding like a 4th of July display of wonder and awe. God loved me and I was happy. It was not until many years later that I discovered that somehow I had missed the true message of the song, *"Just as I am, I come."*

Raised by two working-class parents who struggled to put food on the table meant that, at the end of the day, they were often bone-tired and weary and seldom had the energy (or the will) to encourage and praise their young daughter. I learned very early that if I wanted acceptance and approval, I had to perform some amazing feats to merit their attention. So, as a survival technique, I mastered the art of perfectionism. Having great grades was not enough—the honor society was a must. Having friends was not enough—I needed the popularity of my peers to feed my starving ego. Having a fantastic husband was not enough—I worked to make my marriage perfect (whatever that means). Same struggle in raising my sons—I wanted them to be perfectly dressed and well-mannered (at all times). My home needed to look like a picture from "Better Homes & Gardens" (at all times). You get the picture—I was working myself ragged trying in vain to "feel" accepted and loved. Being "okay" was never an option.

Years later, I began to experience angina so severe that it merited a trip to my family physical who suggested that I needed to relax and adjust my schedule to include downtime (what a concept). I became still enough to hear God (Who had probably been shouting all along) whisper once again to me, this time pleading, "Rest. The only work you are required to do is to give your utmost attention to my voice." And He said, "I love you *just as you are*," and tears of relief flooded my parched soul once again. My prayer is that you will discover that God loves *You just as you are*. He really does!

In the beginning God (prepared,
formed, fashioned, and) created the
heavens and the earth.

—Genesis 1:1

(Amplified)

Joy in the Morning

Hello Friend,

Our God is a Divine Designer. He created an orderly, stable world and methodically filled it with plants and fruit trees. This was a systematic process, separating light from darkness and water from land, naming things as He creates them, and declaring them good. As you study Genesis, you will find patterns and structure and flow. And His crowning achievement was the creation of human beings. "God said, Let Us [Father, Son, and Holy Spirit.]make mankind in Our image, after Our likeness" (v. 26, Amplified). "And God saw everything that he had made, and behold, it was very good (suitable, pleasant) and He approved it completely." (v. 31, Amplified).

The Divine Designer who created the universe fashioned you. I love Psalm 139:13, "For You did form my inward parts; You did knit me together in my mother's womb." (Amplified). God carefully chose your height, your hair color, and set your beautiful eyes in just the right position, making you a unique, one-of-a-kind creation. His hand didn't slip and He didn't become distracted. He carefully formed and fashioned you and declared you good and approved of you completely! Wow! And even more, He created you for a purpose; He has a plan for your life. "For I know the thoughts and plans that I have for you, says the Lord, thoughts and plans for welfare and peace and not for evil, to give you hope . . ." (Jeremiah 29:11, Amplified). This should be our goal and purpose in life—to discover God's plan for us. And His plan is simple: He wants us to have a relationship with Him—to fall madly in love with Him. What a joy to know in your heart of heart that you are a special creation of the Most High God. He didn't make you ordinary—He made you extraordinary. In the bustle of your day, hold that thought in your heart and cherish it.

Feeling special and deeply loved,
Linda

The Optional Element

THE KEYS TO DEVELOPING
A SUCCESSFUL PRAYER LIFE

*Discover the Missing Elements that will Focus
and Motivate Your Life in Prayer*

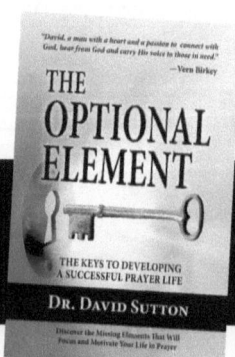

THE CALL TO PRAYER

Everybody is looking for something.

So here I am in Lynden, Washington in the middle of August and it is in the high 60's today. Seeing how the rest of the country is in a heatwave it is notable.

In many ways Lynden is like dropping back in time. A community built around dairy farms, blueberry and raspberry fields, a place where everyone seems to know everyone or is at least friendly to everyone. This little town where there is a church on every street and no real taverns, is situated about 5 minutes from the border crossing to Canada. Sunday most of the stores are closed and family seems to be the focus no matter what you are doing.

I recently attended the Great Northwest Washington Fair in Lynden. This event in this town is about family. There are children everywhere and as fairs go it is clean and pleasant. From the afternoon horse shows to the demolition derby it is all about the family doing this together. Amidst the vast animal barns (more than you could believe) the buildings filled with displays from collections to baked goods, and mostly home grown food, is a little stage area that provides entertainment of all sorts. Singers, comedians (family friendly), jugglers and the like filled, with pithy humor and good fun. You can pass the time under the giant shade trees eating wonderful BBQ and homemade pie. Most of the time you can find a seat even durning the show as people casually stroll in and out.

One event that is different is the Hypnotist Show. In most ways it is like any other fair side show, with the exception that it is packed out for every show, 3 times a day. Every seat is full, people are sitting on the ground and standing room only around the outside of the bleacher style seating. Most shows in this setting draw 150 or so, but this hypnotist has 300 or more audience members for every show. What is the draw? Something beyond the natural and explainable. It doesn't matter if your perception is that it is real or fake, people are drawn to the supernatural. Consider the Harry Potter craze. In this sleepy little town where there is a church on every corner the hunger for the supernatural is still huge!

Are you aware that a large portion of the society we live in, not just in Lynden, are drawn to and even actively looking for something supernatural? People want something real! Something that they can see, feel, touch or experience.

So it is with the church. There is a void that we are looking to fill. We grab anything and everything to fill the void. We discovered that once we have attended all the conferences, heard all the great speakers and sang all the latest worship tunes, the void didn't go away. Nothing in the natural can fill this void. So the supernatural is sought out. The short lived side show event will not ever fill the need. Hearing from someone who heard from God, as wonderful as it is, won't fill the longing either; at least not for long. For those trying to experience the supernatural intervention of a personal God, once they find the real thing, it is all that will ever satisfy the void.

So let me ask you, "Are you living in as much God reality as you desire or is something missing?" Jesus said, "Greater works than these shall you do". What about you? Are you in the greater works mode yet?

Don't ever settle for the slight of hand spirituality, when you can have the real thing. So the call to prayer is about finding the real thing, something that works. If you have had enough of the same old excuses why there is not the power and manifestation of God in your life, that you read about in the Bible, then step up and answer the call. As we start off, let me give you some basics about the call from God to you to pray.

The call to pray is going to always be greater than the response to that call. No matter how great your passion is, or how well you have developed your personal prayer life, the call will be greater. This call will grow in proportion to what you are doing with it, if you remember the scripture that gave us the principle of being faithful with the little so we can become ruler over much. "His lord said unto him, Well done, [thou] good and faithful servant: thou hast been faithful over a few things, I will make thee ruler over many things: enter thou into the joy of thy lord." Matthew 25:21 Before you can ever realize substantial growth in your prayer life, you will need to be faithful with a small prayer life. Most people are not faithful and remain frustrated with the whole matter of prayer.

The call to pray grows in proportion to what you're doing with it. If you only have a prayer life designed to keep you in good standing with God and not with the intention of making a difference in the world where you live, your prayer life won't grow much. It is kind of like the goldfish in the bowl. The fish won't grow any bigger than his surroundings. Use small bowl and the fish will stay small. Put the same fish in a giant aquarium and he will size up. Your prayer life will stay the size of your surrounding vision for the things of God.

The call to pray will often be outside your human understanding. If you consider the limitlessness of God and try to capture it into your comparatively finite understanding of things, your ability to comprehend the things of God will always be a challenge. If you place your limited understanding into the vastness of God's Spirit, your limited human understanding will be empowered.

I'm reminded of a time when I was called to pray for this couple living in an openly ungodly lifestyle. They were clearly living outside the boundaries that I understand to be God's order. However, I prayed for them because I had the prompting of the Spirit in my heart to do so. I was continually troubled by all that I knew about the manner that they lived their life. They were living so far from Biblical standards, I was pretty sure that God would not act on their behalf. As it would be, God healed both of them in a rather miraculous way. I was actually surprised at the healing, to say the least.

As I
Am

A TRUE STORY OF ADAPTATION
TO PHYSICAL DISABILITY

By Garret Lee Frey
and Dr. Karen Hutchins Pirnot

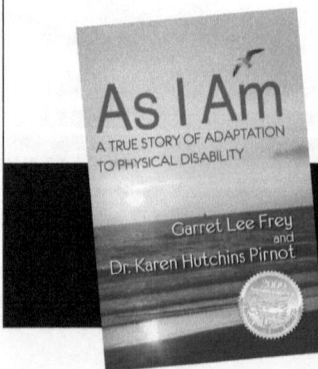

Chapter One

I do not remember the day I was born and I do not remember
the day that I died. I only remember my life As I Am.

It was April 24, 1987 and I had no premonition of the moment in time that would forever alter my conceptualization of my family, myself and the world at large. I was delighted when my father appeared at the home of my babysitter with his motorcycle rather than his unreliable used car, which was frequently in the shop for repairs. Dad had occasionally taken my older brother Kevin and me on the cycle around the block, always being meticulous about our wearing helmets and abiding by all the rules of cycle riding. This would be the longest ride I'd ever taken on that motorcycle, one mile from the home of my babysitter to my own home. But, I never arrived home that day.

Dad greeted me warmly as I ran to him and jumped up into his arms. He put my jacket on me and we said our good-byes to the sitter. We walked to the cycle in the driveway and Dad placed me on the large seat and put on my helmet. Then, I remembered that I had forgotten my favorite yellow blanket and Dad went in to retrieve my trusty security companion. It was somewhat windy and chilly so Dad wrapped the blanket around my neck for extra warmth, tying the ends so that the blanket would remain securely in place and tucked inside my jacket. He then got up on his seat and with one more look, assured himself that I was safe and secure. I reached out and put my arms around his waist and the cycle was started up.

As a nearly five-year-old boy, I loved the feeling of the wind on my face, ready to explore the world around me. I was a hands-on explorer who loved each and every one of my god-given senses. We roared down the street and neither of us thought of anything other than the freedom of the open road. I was in seventh heaven!

I tried to visualize what I would do when we arrived home. I loved to play in our back yard which was lined with evergreens. The trees had such a fresh and inviting aroma. For as long as I can remember, I vowed to live each and every day to the fullest and that day was no different. My mind raced with possibilities.

One of the things that always pleased me was to help others. I helped my mother in the kitchen and I always took pride in helping her to keep it spotless. I also remember helping my father fix his old car so that it would run for yet another day.

If the weather was nice, we would cook hotdogs and hamburgers outside on the grill. I loved the hamburgers, but I always got strange

Garret Lee Frey one year old

Garret with pet dog Chelsea

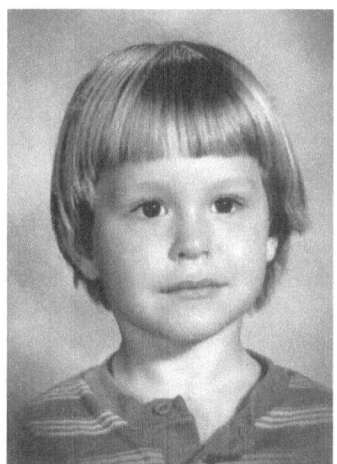

Garret checking out a goat   *Garret Lee Frey age 2*

sensations with the raw meat on my hands before it was put onto the grill. It was my job to add the seasonings, and then, to watch the burgers cook just the right amount. I always mentally picked out my own burger and was delighted when no one else picked it up first.

Those who knew our family would probably say that I was somewhat of a mama's boy as I tended to gravitate toward her when the family gathered. When I sat on her lap watching television programs, I always had my favorite blanket which had a special silky tag on the edge of the fabric. I remember rubbing it between my fingers and holding it as I sucked my thumb. That was always a relaxing and safe feeling.

If Mom was at work, Dad would be at home to fix dinner. Sometimes, after we ate, we'd watch movies together. I remember loving the movies Top Gun and Gremlins. Even though they were scary movies for a young child, I had an older brother who loved them and I imagine that I wanted to show him that I was not a little sissy brother.

Poetry

FACING THE SEA
Selected Poems
PIERRE CHATILLON

FROZEN SYMMETRY
VICKI MICKELSON

Meet Me in the Moment
Lisa Shenouda Koslow

HOW DOES TRUTH TRAVEL?
Stories, Poems and Essays
NANCY RUSSO WILSON

EXCAVATIONS
Twenty Oedipal Prose Poems
HAROLD WOLFE

THE WIZARDS

I like the wizards
During their lifetime they go
From village to village
On cloud-pink horses
They are not wild animal tamers
They free people from their cages
They make a dove
Pop out of the black hat of misfortune
And change itself into a flower
From a flying trapeze
They jump into space
Go around the moon
Then come back to earth
Aureoled with a golden halo
Spectacular fire-eaters
They plunge suns into their throats
And their translucent bodies shine

FACING
THE
SEA

PIERRE CHATILLON

That they change
Into love poems
Tightrope walkers of the soul
High up in their dream
On an invisible wire
They walk above time
They are not
Simple knife throwers
They have in their quivers
Long arrows of light
They draw tight on the azure
Rainbows
And shoot their arrows
Over the night
And at the end
They jump through
Death's burning hoop
And fall straight
Into eternity

SOMETIMES I RECEIVE LETTERS

Sometimes I receive letters
From the child I was
Adorned with stamps representing
The sun
He writes to me from over the seas
But these are not earthly seas
He encloses with his missives
Drawings of clouds and planets
His envelopes are delivered by the wind
I find them on the beach
Wetted by the waves
Then the pages slip out of my hands
And fly away
I know he is happy somewhere on an island
He tells me that he plays in the water
With boat-shaped pieces of wood
But it is not an earthly isle

Meet Me in the Moment

Lisa Shenouda Koslow

I Am the Desert Dust

I am the desert dust, dry and dispersed, blown here and there
in random patterns.

I am the hieroglyphs that my ancestors used to write down their lives,
their stories, as now I write mine.

I am the waters of the Nile, flowing smoothly and softly, while seeking
refuge at land's edge.

I am my mother and my father living on, with new dreams much like
the ones that brought them here, so many years ago.

I am an altered version of myself, each day, this day, as change
surrounds me and calls me, asking me to meet it, at least halfway.

My poet friend, Nan

A neighbor for so many years
long lost moons ago in our northern Long Island land
she now spans the country in distant Arizona
where dryness and strange creatures live
alongside beautiful mountains she loves to climb

Her home comes with a view
her life lived in rich texture with spouse, friends and meaning
as she counsels and teaches and easily takes her yoga pose
contemplating life's journey with its quirks and turns
for better or worse

Twenty years in that "foreign land"
my visits have numbered just two while I still wait for her one
as our friendship sits on computer screens
filled with thoughts and dreams

Our past easily remembered with dinners and backyard idylls
the present shared in words and their craft
forging a strong link despite the years

It's a very good thing.

The Music of Water

I can still hear the "music of water"
as it laps against the rocks
whistling between crevices
dancing with the sea wind
while I stand nearby on shore

Other days I am deeply into the water
hearing the "music of water"
now strangely somber, quietly muffled
as I swim below the sun's shadow
weaving wondrously between each wave

Those long ago summer forays
stay with me still as I now walk alone
along the warm water's edge
a horizon in sight of the setting sun
hearing the "music of water"

FROZEN
SYMMETRY

VICKI MICKELSON

CONCEPT REALIZED

I knew the moment of conception

It was crystal clear

The swimmers had united

In full force

Breast stroking with muscled fins

The warm canal

Filled with green lights

And guiding tubal turrets

Urging them upward

An explosion

Like a Fourth of July firecracker

Illuminating the sky

They imploded

Sliding up the backsplash

Surfacing to catch

The flirty chick

In the gold lame'

Bathing suit

Diving in

Sans a bathing cap

Strands of her blond ponytail
Easing her chin
Down a slippery slope
Like a bunny in a mud hole
Suffocated by an entanglement
Of frothy scales and limbs
Too close to the bottom drain
Sucked through
Framing a jelly fish
Grasping for pulsating flesh
Forming a nurtured bean
Cradled but insecure
In a fertile film of dreams

FEELIN GOOD

Finally a pregnancy
With no morning sickness
I was ecstatic
No clearing the shelves
At Red Owl of Sunshine saltines
No more flinging the car door open
At stop signs to puke
No more three-inch stack of tissues
Folded neatly in a purse pocket
No more dizzy weavings
Under Target's fluorescent lights
No more emergency exits
To the teachers' lounge
It was obvious my insides
Were behaving nicely
Aside from swollen breasts
I didn't feel with child
Glorious
To be full of bursting seed
And anticipation

HOW DOES TRUTH TRAVEL?

Stories, Poems and Essays

NANCY RUSSO WILSON

POEMS

*Let us tenderly and kindly cherish
the means of knowledge,
let us dare to read, to think,
to speak, to write.*

*John Adams (1735 - 1826)
2nd American President, Founding Father – USA*

A WALK IN CENTRAL PARK

Central Park, New York City 10/12

+ Small paths over old stone bridges, carved with curlicues and florets, their patterns cast shadows on the ground, covered with acorns.

+ Looking down at the path as I circle the reservoir I see a bit of glitter, it is an earring. I think some fast-running woman has lost it among the leavews which line the grass edge. I wonder if she misses it.

THE MIRROR

Sarasota 04/13

I talk to my reflection a lot. I make serious faces, goofy faces. Sometimes I see pain, other times I see anger.

I tell the person looking back at me to smile, and I look pretty.

I comfort the worried woman and tell her "This too shall pass" and I count my blessings.

I give myself advice and I also chide myself. I can be whoever or however I want to be.

When I look in the mirror I always see a true friend. I can make myself laugh.

I always understand this person before me. She is with me always.

WORDS MATTER

Ithaca 08/14

The word is *carry*. What does it mean?

To bear	To ferry	To spirit
To sway	To yield	To sail
To drift	To transport	

You cannot carry sentiment or negativity with you if you seek truth and love nature.

Flowers in a Pond

Zentangle is making lines and figures, a free-form style of meditation -

Patterns bubble up to the surface much like petals of sea lilies in a pond -

The lines, circles, shadows, triangles transfer to the water like written ripples of oleander and palm leaves –

Designs of motion and spirit, red roses among the lilies.

Stones and Rocks

Along the lakeshore, I see a rock – I see a bird or an animal in the curves, shape, formations – I paint the image, the rock speaks – it is timeless.

I see smooth round river stones, I paint words on them, "love," "mercy," "grace," "truth," "spirit," "God," "life," "faith," hope."

I find a scripture with the word on the rock. I write the scripture on a fine piece of linen – I wrap the rock in a soft ribbon – I give it to someone.

I am simply a messenger, the rock comes from eternity. A child could make a game out of this – I would call this game Scripture Stones. All of Nature could play with us.

EXCAVATIONS
Twenty Oedipal Prose Poems

By

Harold Wolfe

III

Roots

These things are clear to me now.

That as the oak must sway
before the raging winds of nature,
so I must bend before the storms
that swirl deep within my inner life.

That as a poet, I am compelled to tell
a tale arising from my early memories,
my dreams, my fantasies.

That many poems of mine are rooted in past feelings,
feelings of the injured child that still resides in me,
feelings that still work their way into my daily life,
feelings to which I must give written form, continually,
in order to preserve the soundness of my searching mind.

VI

First Session

When we first met, fear lurked,
like a tiger, behind my eyes.
Helplessness enveloped me like a lead net.
Close to hopelessness, I stood
at the edge of an abyss,
looking down at nothingness,
wanting only to escape
the terror that was nearly paralyzing me.

VII

The Digger

He digs in the coal pits of the mind.
Picks and shovels, then uncovers
primal urges: coupling, killing;
evil wishes, incestuous and patricidal;
fluctuating filial love and hate,
and the rending, sometimes crippling,
tugs of war that they engender.

All this labor leaves the digger aching,
choking on the dust and, without warning, sobbing.

Young Readers

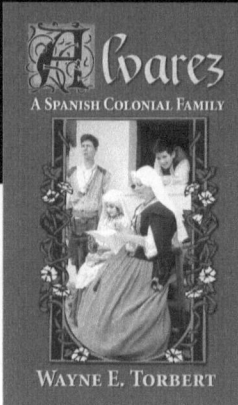

Chapter 1

At last, the long day was done, and it was time for Papa to tell me a bedtime story. My sister Mercedes and I always looked forward to the special treat of my father's stories at bedtime.

It was an October evening in 1703, and the days were getting shorter and the nights cooler. My family had finished a light supper of pumpkin bread with butter. Mama had put her spinning wheel away, and Papa had put his work to the side. He was a tailor, perhaps the best one at Mission San Luis.

Papa enjoyed telling a good story. Many of his tales were of history, but sometimes his imagination soared and he would give the story a funny twist. It was the best part of the day for me.

Did I mention that my sister was nine years old, and I would be turning twelve in mid-November? Anyway, Papa pulled up a stool next to the bed, and we gave him our full attention.

"Tonight I will tell you how Florida got its name. It all started when the Governor of Puerto Rico, Ponce de Leon, heard a tale about a magical fountain that would restore one's youth. The Fountain of Youth was in a land somewhere to the north of Puerto Rico. Can you imagine how wonderful it would be to discover a spring of eternal youth, where all you had to do was sip its water and your youth was restored? Well, when Ponce de Leon heard about this fountain, he became determined to find it."

Papa continued with the story. "So, many men agreed to help him find this magical fountain. They sailed to the northwest, where they found some small islands that we now call the Bahamas. Continuing north, they landed at a place which today we know as St. Augustine. It was April 1513, during the Easter Season, which is known as the Festival of Flowers, so it was only natural that Ponce de Leon should call this new land, La Florida, the Land of Flowers."

"Papa, did Ponce de Leon find his Fountain of Youth?" I asked.

"Well, now, he found a spring at this place. He took a drink of the cool waters and to the amazement of his men he became younger and younger right before their eyes, until he was just a little baby cradled in the armor he had been wearing."

"Ha! Papa, is that true?" I asked in wonder.

"Juan, I must confess, I made up that last part. No, he did find a good spring, but it didn't have the magical power to restore one's youth."

"Is there really a Fountain of Youth, then?" asked Mercedes.

Papa thought for a moment, and then said, "So far, nobody has found this fountain of legend, yet we know that magic does exist in the world, and perhaps someday the fountain will be found."

"Now, say your bedtime prayers and go to sleep, my little ones," said Papa.

After my sister and I said our prayers, Mama tucked us in and wished us a good night.

"*Buenes noches*, Mama," we replied.

The crowing of our rooster woke me. It was the first chilly morning of the autumn season, and I wanted to stay warm under the blanket. Mama had started a fire in the brazier, and as the room gradually warmed up I finally slipped out of bed. My sister and I huddled close to the brazier to get warm. I thought to myself, when I grow up I'm going to build my house with a fireplace and chimney just the way Papa said the English do.

"Children, please, take care of the chickens," said Mama.

Each night the chickens are locked up in the chicken coop to protect them from hungry foxes. Our first chore of the day is to let them out and gather the eggs for breakfast. My sister and I work as a team to achieve this goal. While I feed the chickens, Mercedes will go into the chicken coop and retrieve the hens' eggs, placing them carefully in her basket.

"Mama, we got six eggs for breakfast today!" exclaimed

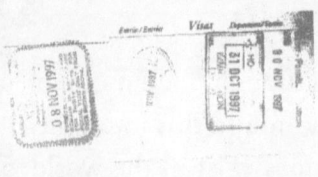

Abby & GG Get Going

A 21st Century Grand Tour

by

April Gamble

London,
England

"Are you all set, Cupcake"?

"Passport, IPad, and gummy bears, all ready." I gave my Dad a playful salute.

My little sister loves stuffed toys, so when Penny handed over her favorite stuffed bear to take along I considered that a very generous departure gift. My backpack was already pretty full, but I set it on the floor and stuffed the teddy inside, then gave my sister a big kiss.

"Thank you, Lollypop, I am going to miss you." GG once told me she liked the fact that there was six years' difference in the ages of her granddaughters. She would be able to travel alone with me for a number of years, and when I am a teenager and probably more interested in spending my free time with my friends, she could then begin travelling with Penny to all of the places she had shown me. To GG this idea provided many years of happy travel anticipation. The problem with that theory is I cannot imagine not wanting to take trips with her, and I also know if in the future I want to bring a friend along she will probably say yes.

Today I was at LAX. The first thing I have to do when I leave California is get on a huge plane. It holds about 350 people. My Dad usually drives me to Los Angeles because he insists on no plane changes. I am glad, because that would be kind of scary.

"Have a great time with your grandmother, but remember not to get dragged into any of her ..."

"Misunderstandings, Dad?"

"Yeah, Cupcake, those," he said with slight sarcasm.

My Dad had told me he knew from firsthand experience world travel is very useful in showing, not just telling, what makes other people and cultures different, but more importantly what makes them the same. He was pleased with my grandmother's good intentions, but less so at some of the outcomes.

GG was always optimistic and often told me she was proud of her tutelage provided by our travels and we should not allow the occasional misunderstanding that had cropped up along the way to dampen our enthusiasm. Works for me.

I have already been to many places, but the Grand Tour was just GG and I. Today we were headed to Switzerland.

GG had wanted to take me to Cairo, Egypt, to see the pyramids and that sounded amazing, but my parents said at this time it was not safe. So instead, GG decided on Switzerland, which she felt the lakes and the Matterhorn would be a huge contrast to big cities and the small coastal town of Santa Barbara. I was excited to see what this new place had to offer. The only Matterhorn I had ever seen was at Disneyland.

I gave my Dad another big goodbye kiss. When I said goodbye again to Penny she started to cry.

"No, Abby, don't go away. I want you to stay with me and Daddy." Now she was even louder. My Dad picked her up and gave her a cuddle and a big wink to me.

"Daddy, can I have a Hello Kitty book?" was the last thing I heard as I walked with my escort through the security door.

The plane ride is long and boring, and I usually just watch DVDs and eat ice cream until I get sleepy. I get to fly first class because GG has loads of frequent flyer miles. I think she gets them from buying all those shoes.

After just about forever I arrived at my first stop: Heathrow Airport in London, England. This is where GG and I meet up.

This place is gigantic and noisy. As I made my way up the long ramp, a lady with a huge purse ran her wheelie bag right over my foot. "Ouch" just popped out of my mouth. I looked right at her, expecting her to say excuse me or sorry, but she didn't say anything. Then she scowled at me as if I owed her an apology.

I wanted to say "Hey lady, I am just a kid, but I know when someone is being rude." But I didn't say anything and just kept walking.

You have to walk and walk and walk to get out of the building, which I don't mind after I have been sitting on a plane for eleven and a half hours. That is right, eleven-plus long hours. That is like two full school days in a row with no recess.

I have been at this airport before, but it is always a confusing place so I am really glad there is an airline escort to help me.

Passport Control is my first stop and is where each country

THE YOMY TALES
An American Experience

Carol Marie Davis

Illustrated by the Author

CHAPTER ONE
1850- On a Plantation in Maryland

"She's my Yomy!"

"She's not yours, she's my Yomy!"

The twins Gracie and Goodie were at it again; tossing me and my sister back and forth and mixing us up so they couldn't tell one doll from the other. It's true that my sister and I look alike; we even have the same name, which came from saying "yours" and "my" often enough that it became shortened to just Yomy for the both of us. But I am older; I am the first dolly their mama Maebelle created.

Right after she made me, I watched Maebelle put together my sister Yomy. To begin with, she stuffed an old stocking with cotton to make a head, body and limbs and then sewed on some strands of yarn for hair. She found two shiny shoe buttons for her eyes, and, as a finishing touch, she embroidered a cute crooked little smile on Yomy's face, a feature that has always made my sister so endearing.

On the day that our little mamas Gracie and Goodie were tossing us around, their Grandmama Mo Mary could stand no more of their prankish behavior.

"Children, stop fussing with your dollies now!" she said out loud, taking Yomy and me away and placing us high on a shelf out of the girls' reach.

"It is going to rain today so you better stay inside and be useful; sweep the cabin and prepare the corn meal for supper," she said wagging her finger at them.

From my perch on the shelf, I could see Goodie and Gracie frown and stick out their lower lips but they knew better than to talk back to their grandmamma. She loved them dearly but was known to spank their behinds with a strong hand if they disobeyed.

Despite the cloudy skies, the elderly woman headed out to the tobacco fields, for she was one of many African American slaves living on the Harris Blood plantation forced to work six days a week, rain or shine.

"It's boring in here," said Goodie after Mo Mary closed the door of one-room cabin in the slave's quarters where they lived.

Indeed, the place was dreary even when the sun shone, but when the sky clouded over like it did that day, such a tiny speck of light entered their one window that only the flames in the fireplace chased away the gloom.

"I know what we can do," said Gracie. "We can get our Yomys down and play with them now that Grandmama's gone."

Goodie wasted no time shoving a chair against the wall and grabbing us off the shelf. Then, sure enough, they continued their mischief, subjecting our soft little bodies to lots of tugging and pulling while they dressed and undressed us countless times.

Now please don't get me wrong, dear reader, our little mamas loved us a lot for they also kissed and hugged us so much that we looked a little flattened like a pancake in a skillet.

By noontime that day, the threatening rain broke through the clouds and poured down in torrents. It seeped through the cabin's flimsy board roof, slid down the log walls chinked with mud and created quite a mess on the earth floor. To my astonishment the girls did not seem to mind all this until Gracie slipped and fell while trying to take me away from Goodie. She slammed into her sister and down we tumbled onto the muddy floor.

As if getting covered with dirt wasn't bad enough, the next thing that happened was terrifying- heavy rain swooshed through a newly-formed hole in the ceiling and then Bam! Boom! Bang! The cabin roof caved in around us.

At first the girls sat there stunned. "Are you ok?" asked Goodie feeling her arms and legs for broken bones.

"I guess I'm alright except for some scratches," replied Gracie. Before I could get my bearings, the girls opened their mouths wide and screamed for help at the top of their lungs.

Now it was a good thing that old Aunt Ida who lived next door heard the racket and ran out of her cabin lickety-split. Every other person, you see, was far away working in the wet fields.

"My Goodness, Gracious! Come on out of that broken-down house right away," Aunt Ida scolded, reaching in to help both girls to their feet. Once inside the cabin, she made them go to a

BAYOCOR'S ADVENTURES

THE OLD CARRIAGE HOUSE

by Su Gerheim

CHAPTER 1

Bayocor followed Jake as far as the chain-link fence at the side of the house. The puppy barked and paced back and forth when Jake closed the gate, leaving him behind. *Jake, come back!* the puppy thought. The ten-year-old boy, Bay's best friend, waved goodbye to him. "See ya later, Bay," he said.

The five-month-old Labrador had to stay home while Jake attended a safety class at the fire station. Mom and Dad had said Bay would be in the way. The class taught children about the dangers and prevention of fires, and attending it was one part of Jake's making good for starting a fire in a cave in the forest a month ago. Another part was Bay helping the boy clean out an old barn behind the fire station that housed an antique horse-drawn fire carriage. The puppy liked going to the fire station. The firefighters greeted him with happy smiles and scratches behind the ears. He liked their four-year-old Dalmatian, Dotty, too. She was the first to greet him and Jake with energetic, excited barks and lots of doggie-kisses. The yellow Labrador laughed to himself. *Her tail wags so hard,* he thought, *half her body swishes back and forth.*

The puppy pushed through the bushes between his backyard and his friend Dodger's backyard. He thought about all the trouble he and his buddy, Jake, had gotten into last month. *My shoulder feels like new now. It doesn't hurt as much as it did when we came out of that cave. What a scary animal a bear is. Jake sure got into trouble that day, but I'm glad my bandage is gone. It got itchy.*

He looked up into George's favorite maple tree. Sure enough, the old tomcat who lived with Dodger snoozed away, his front paw hanging over the branch. Leaves twisted and sparkled in the sun when the breeze blew through them. "Come down and play, George," Bayocor said.

George lifted his head, yawned, and stretched his front paws. "No thanks, Sonny. I'm just fine right here. I don't like chasing my tail. I'll stay here and watch for dangers. That's my kind of exercise. I'll let you know if I see anything."

Bay blinked. "Okay, but that sounds boring to me." *Danger—how can he see anything with his eyes shut?* Bay wondered.

Dodger, his long hair hanging over his eyes, popped out from behind a shed in the corner of the backyard, a long branch in his mouth. Bay tilted his head and watched him struggle to drag the branch across the lawn.

George looked down at Dodger and shook his head. The branch was twice as long as the Skye terrier and he walked sideways to drag it. Bay ran to the other end of it and grabbed it in his mouth. The two wobbled and weaved across the yard, tugging back and forth until Dodger dropped his end and sped off toward his house.

Bay flinched and stopped, still holding the branch. His eyes tracked his friend's quick movements. Bay dragged the branch a few more steps, then dropped it. "Where are you going?" he said.

"Something ran under the deck," Dodger said.

"Gee whiz, boy. You're a fidgety dog," George said. "There's nothing under the deck. I'd have seen it long before it got close."

"I thought I saw something move," Dodger said.

"Yeah, it's the butterfly you see flying around your head," George said, "or maybe it's just your imagination."

Trade Books

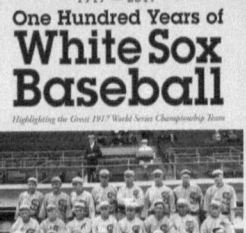

✦ Chapter 1

By George, "I Think You've Got It"

"A mighty flame followeth a tiny spark."

Dante

The Birth and Evolution of
Martial Arts of the Mind for Teachers

THE BEGINNING

My first college class in education would ignite a spark that would produce a lasting flame in my career as a teacher. The professor started this class by posing the following question, "Twenty years from now, will you be a teacher who has twenty years of experience, or a teacher who taught one year twenty times?"

Martial Arts
of the Mind
for Teachers

An Arsenal of Powerful Approaches
to Combat Teachers' Daily Challenges

Paul T.Morelli

This focus, along with an innate hunger to perform at a very high level, stayed with me throughout my 32 years in education. Learning became a lifetime pursuit.

THE POWER OF A CUP OF COFFEE

During the time I was taking this education class, I would soon discover that having a simple cup of coffee in the student center could prove to be an equally important event. On a Monday morning at 7:30, I was having a cup of coffee with my friend, George, who was a student in my study group. We were discussing an assignment for the upcoming class. A student named Mike, who was sitting at a table behind us, grabbed George from behind and attempted to put him in a choke hold. Coffee and coffee cups went flying everywhere. Now, George had Mike in a choke hold. While in this painful and compromising position, Mike apologized and claimed that he was just fooling around. It was quite obvious that he was trying to show off to his friends. George, slowly and gently released Mike. There was complete silence in that area of the student center for the next few moments. Without saying anything, everyone got up and headed to their 8:00 class.

While having lunch with George later that day, we discussed the unfortunate incident that occurred in the student center. Upon questioning him about his instant response to Mike's aggression, he credited it to the training he had in both the armed forces and in karate. Although I thought that the speed and power of his technique was extraordinary, George claimed that it was merely a standard self-defense technique. He didn't think it was such a big deal.

However, there was something other than George's speed and technique that was even more impressive—it was George's attitude and disposition. He stayed cool, calm, and was under control during this entire episode. George didn't make a big deal of it. Instead he got an unsuspecting attacker under control and then showed his attacker compassion by releasing him. I believe George was able to do this, because he didn't seem to possess fear. At no time did George grandstand or brag— instead, he had a humble attitude. That really impressed the heck out of me.

THE BIRTH OF MARTIAL ARTS OF THE MIND FOR TEACHERS

The more that I reflected on the incident in the student center, the more it seemed profound. It was obvious to me that George was a very confident individual who possessed superior physical skills. His focus was like a powerful laser beam and nothing seemed to alter, distract, or impede it.

He also displayed some exemplary character traits, such as humility, fearlessness, compassion and kindness. All these skills and traits were demonstrated instantaneously in the face of adversity. George had the total package of physical skills along with some very impressive character traits.

This response was something some people may preach about, but it was the first time that I witnessed such an extraordinary event. Instantly, I experienced a deep desire to possess all these traits and skills. This was what I needed to enable me become a better teacher.

As teachers, it is our responsibility to stay calm, cool and collected. Quality teachers try never to intentionally lose their temper. The incident in the student center, along with

POPULAR MUSICS

A SHORT HISTORY
2ND EDITION

ALICE A. MOERK
COVER AND ILLUSTRATIONS BY JOAN PETERS

CHAPTER ONE

THE ANCIENT WORLD

Great Goddess sing, which did the Greeks engage
In many woes and mighty Hero's Ghosts
Sent down untimely to the Stygian Coasts[1]

Opportunities for play and entertainment were found in Near-Eastern civilizations, but life in the ancient world was brief and cultural activities were not primary.

Few examples survive of popular music prior to the Middle Ages. There are early artistic remnants of music-making among the Sumerians, and more concerning the Hebrews and Egyptians. It is the Greek and Roman civilizations, however, that left enough of a legacy that the modern world may speak with some certainty of their cultures.

GREECE

Greek society was aristocratic. The number of noble families and freemen was extensive in proportion to slaves: freemen outnumbered slaves by 2:1 in Athens, the largest of the city-states.[2] The majority of the populace was thus well-to-do and well-informed, and the duties of slaves permitted citizens considerable amounts of leisure time.

---

1   John Ogilby, **Homer, His Iliads Translated** (1660), Creative Commons Attribute-ShareAlike License.
2   C. M. Bowra, **The Greek Experience** (NY: Mentor, 1957), 85-86.

Music itself held a dual meaning in Greek thought. It was "... the whole of intellectual or literary culture as opposed to the culture of the bodily faculties [gymnastics] ... [and] the dance movements which accompany singing, and the poetic text itself."[3] Music, as we know it, was a secondary concern to the literature of the era. It was not self-contained, but closely allied to poetry and dance. Each of the three was considered both a craft and divinely inspired.

Several terms applied to the arts, but there was no specific word for any of them. *Sophiâ* denoted skill or wisdom and was a term applied to all of the fine arts. *Poêsis* meant making, *epos* was the term for epic, *soidê* referred to song, and *molpê* signified a combination of song and dance.[4] An *aoidos* was a singer who accompanied himself on the lyre; *rhapsodes* were the reciters of epic poems who traveled throughout Greece with their long staffs.[5]

The Greeks had an intricate scalar system that was later transferred to the church modes of the Middle Ages. Their sense of music varied between city-states. The Dorian culture of Sparta had a strong community life and emphasized choral music; the Ionian culture of Attica (including Athens) stressed individualism and a large portion of its music was soloistic.

Similarly, an ethical and ethnic character was ascribed to Greek scales. The Dorian portended strength and manliness; the Phrygian represented ecstasy and passion, the Lydian was sensed as feminine and lascivious and the Mixolydian felt as sad and mournful.[6] Greek audiences tacitly understood that the poetry and music that comprised

3   Translated from T. Reinach, art. "Musica" in **Dictionnaire des antiquités greques et romaines**, Vol. III, p. 2072, and quoted in Gustave Reese, **Music in the Middle Ages** (NY: Norton, 1940), 11.

4   Bowra, 135-136.

5   H. L. Baldry, **Ancient Greek Literature in its Living Context** (NY: McGraw-Hill, 1968), 25.

6   These can be sensed by using white notes on a keyboard: C-c – Ionian, D-d – Dorian, E-e – Phrygian, F-f – Lydian, G-g – Mixolydian.

their song were inspired. The idea of popular appeal was far from their frames of reference.

Many of the lyric solo songs of the poet-musicians from Lesbos – Sappho, Alcaeus, and Anakreon – are thought to derive from much older folk songs; their subjects are ancient and the few surviving examples are simple and direct.[7] A *Song of Seikilos* remains, most likely written during the Augustan age at the turn of the first century. Found on the tombstone of Seikolos' wife, Euterpe, the text reads proverbially:

"As long as you live, be cheerful; do not grieve much and toil too much, for the span of life is short and death reaches you soon."[8]

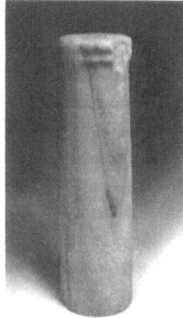

Song of Seikolos   *National Museum of Denmark*

The songwriter emerged early in the fifth century B.C. at the great festivals. Using virtually any excuse – celebration of the harvest, worship of a god, the commemoration of a great victory, the honor of a brave memory – eulogies, choral odes, and hymns were recited in evenings of

---

7   Quoted in Hugo Leichtentritt, **Music, History and Ideas** (Cambridge: Harvard University Press, 1938), 20.

8   Baldry, 30. Several performances of this work can be found on Youtube.

1917 – 2017
One Hundred Years of White Sox Baseball

*Highlighting the Great 1917
World Series Championship Team*

"The Greatest Franchise That Never Was!"

by
Mark Pienkos

with Foreword by Paul Ladewski

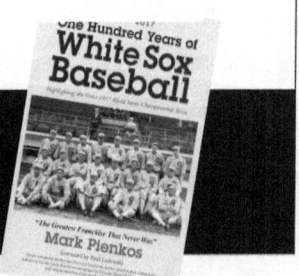

Foreword

By Paul Ladewski

Is there a more tortured, more savvy, more South Side tough person in all of baseball than a White Sox fan?

Say it ain't so, Joe. The damn Yankees. Swoontember of '67. Tito Freaking Landrum. Sosa for Bell. Bevington's reign of error. The strike of '94. Disappointments, White Sox fans got a million of 'em.

Through thin and thinner, though, White Sox fans always come back for more. They're more loyal than a wolf pack. They can find a silver lining in a botched squeeze bunt. They believe a 1-0 count is the start of a rally.

These people are so sick, they're funny, I tell ya.

See, I've known one in particular for a while now.

Mark and I met in high school. We talked ball at lunch tables. Competed in the driveway. Went to college together. Here it is a few million pitches later, and guess who's still hopeful about his Hosers?

Tell you something else about White Sox fans – they're real, not fake. No bandwagon-jumpers here.

White Sox fans like things in black and white, not color. They believe in basics, not curses, black cats and rotten luck. They can tell you the score – and the count, too. They don't just know good baseball. They demand it . . .

Tipton for Fox. The Go-Go Sox. The South Side Hit Men. Wilbur and Dick. The Big Hurt. Winnin' Ugly in '83. Winnin' it all in '05. Memories, White Sox fans got a million of those, too.

(Now should I tell them about that other team in town?)

Paul Ladewski is a sports columnist for the San Francisco Examiner and former sports editor, sportswriter and columnist for the Daily Southtown newspaper in Chicago. As a veteran member of the Baseball Writers Association, Paul is a Baseball Hall of Fame voter. Among his many honors, Paul was the recipient of the Peter Lisagor and Illinois Sports Columnist of the Year awards. In 2014, Paul was selected as the Executive Director for the Chicago Baseball Museum where he has also served as its website editor and correspondent. Paul and Mark became friends during their freshman year at St. Laurence High School in Burbank, Illinois. They also attended Northern Illinois University where they both graduated in 1972. Their friendship extends nearly fifty years!

Chapter One

On Deck

A CENTURY — ONE HUNDRED YEARS — IS A LONG TIME

Let's assume no one is still alive who saw the World Series Champion Chicago White Sox play during the 1917 season. No one from that era is alive to tell the story of how great that 1917 team was. Certainly people over the years have written about some of its players. The most famous is "Shoeless" Joe Jackson whose life has been written about in books and portrayed in movies. One of these books is Eliot Asinof's *Eight Men Out* that details the story of the 1919 Black Sox scandal that saw eight players from the American League pennant-winning Chicago team conspire to throw the World Series against the Cincinnati Reds. I read this book when I was about thirteen or fourteen years old. My brother, Don, gave me a copy.

I remember devouring this book as the 1964 baseball season was about to begin. There were lots of discussions going on in the papers as *Chicago Tribune* and *Sun-Times* sports writers chronicled the prospects of the two Chicago teams – Cubs and Sox – as they got ready to start the season. Although there is still a pretty hefty rivalry between Sox and Cub fans, I think this has mellowed over the years. Not in my family, mind you; but I think it has just changed over time. In fact, today you occasionally hear

THE POVERTY ADVANTAGE

TRANSFORMING HARD TIMES
TO GOOD TIMES

Robert L. Bailey

1.

FLUNKING FIRST GRADE

*Education is what survives when what has been
learned has been forgotten.*

—B. F. Skinner

Ten of us were seated at the big round table: six university deans, two students hand-picked from the
student population, and my wife and I.

"If there were no financial limitations and no political
constraints, what would you do to improve the quality of
education in our country?" I asked. There was silence.
Finally one dean asked, "What do you mean by no financial limitations or political constraints?"

"You can have all the money you need. Use your own
judgment. No taxpayer approval. Neither the politicians
nor the university administration can turn you down," I
answered.

There was more silence. "That's a tough question," another dean said. "We've always felt constrained by money
and politics."

Then one of the students spoke. "We've got to get parents interested and involved in the type of education we
receive," she said. "Students do well when their parents
are interested in the outcome." This young lady believes
quality education is not a money issue but a parent in-
volvement issue, which reminds me that home schooled

kids generally rank among the smartest kids in the country.

Taxpayers in most states are spending $11,000 to $16,000 per student per year for public school education. New Jersey taxpayers are spending $22,000 per student in the Newark school system. Over the past 40 years spending per student has increased 2.6 times (adjusted for inflation) while SAT scores have remained level. Still many young people are not equipped to earn a living, and the reason is often, "We just don't have the money to provide a sound education." In some cases the districts that spend the most produce the greatest number of ill-prepared young people.

The first eight years of my public school education were in a one-room country school in Kansas about a mile from the farm where I was raised. Its official name was District 34, better known as the Custard School, so named because it sat on a plot carved from the old Custard farm. There was no electricity and no running water. Heat was from a huge coal-fired stove. The boys' and girls' outhouses sat at opposite back corners of the one-acre plot. The girls' outhouse had a concrete sidewalk that led to it. The boys had to plod through the snow and mud. The school building still stands today and is used to store hay for a neighboring farmer.

I couldn't wait until I was old enough to go to school. At the end of the school day I would stand at the kitchen window and wait for the "big kids" to walk over the hill east of our house. When I was finally old enough to begin first grade, I was thrilled. Now I was one of the "big kids."

The first grade didn't turn out that well. I failed first grade, but I had good company. Every kid in the entire school failed.

Our teacher was Ula Cox. Of all the teachers I've had in elementary school, high school and college, I can remember most of the very good ones, and all the very bad ones, but I can't remember many of those in the middle. But I do remember Ula Cox.

There were long wooden benches along both sides of the one-room school. Every day following lunch, Miss Cox would lie down on the bench along the north wall of the school and take a nap.

I didn't see anything wrong with a nap after lunch. I thought it was a good idea. I often joke that it was probably a benefit that had been negotiated by the teachers' union.

Although I didn't recognize it at the time, during lunch hour she would allegedly go to her car and take a little nip of whiskey, which may have been warranted. I remember some of those kids in school, and she may have really needed something to soothe her nerves.

I don't recall telling my parents about her little interlude, but somehow the school board heard about her practice and fired her near the end of the school year. She retaliated by turning in to the Bourbon County Kansas Board of Education failing grades for every student in school. Fortunately, all of us made up for our "failure" the following year by taking two grades simultaneously.

Just imagine: one room, one teacher, a six-hour work day, plus a couple of recesses, divided by eight grades. There was little time to spend with any one grade, even without a daily nap for the teacher.

Yet there was an advantage. By the time I got to the eighth grade, I'd been through it seven times. It was like a pre-television version of Sesame Street. We learned through repetition. I hate to brag, but for six of the eight

www.ingramcontent.com/pod-product-compliance
Lightning Source LLC
Chambersburg PA
CBHW050454290526
45786CB00006B/2283